W9-BPQ-217

Seasons of Hope

Seasons of Hope

Readings for the Liturgical Year

David E. Butler

UNITED CHURCH PRESS

Cleveland, Ohio

This collection is dedicated to Maureen Tannian Butler,
my friend, my inspiration, and my wife,
who continues to awaken a new heart in me.

United Church Press, Cleveland, Ohio 44115
© 1998 by David E. Butler

Biblical quotations are from the New Revised Standard Version of the Bible,
© 1989 by the Division of Christian Education of the National Council of
the Churches of Christ in the U.S.A., and are used by permission. Adaptations have been made for inclusive language.

Published 1998. All rights reserved

Printed in the United States of America on acid-free paper

03   02   01   00   99   98   5   4   3   2   1

Library of Congress Cataloging-in-Publication Data

Butler, David E.
    Seasons of hope : readings for the liturgical year / David E. Butler.
        p.   cm.
    ISBN 0-8298-1217-2 (pbk. : alk. paper)
    1. Responsive worship.   2. Church year.   3. Common lectionary
(1992)   I. Title.
BV199.R5B87   1998
242'.2—dc21   98-13953
                                                          CIP

Contents

❧

Acknowledgments

I would like to gratefully acknowledge the help, patience, and forbearance of the members of Trinity Church in Northboro, Weston Congregational Church, and Trinitarian Church in Concord, all in Massachusetts. These people have all listened to these readings, often in more primitive versions, and have offered suggestions, comments, and great encouragement.

Also, a special acknowledgment of the great contribution of my late friend Valerie Russell, who inspired some of the pieces, commissioned some of the others, commented on most, and lovingly supported this endeavor.

Introduction

What follows is a collection of readings intended to be shared aloud during public worship. They have all been tried and used in a variety of worship settings. Many of them are responsive meditations that incorporate a biblical passage: these work well when used in place of one of the scripture readings. All of them are in some way consistent with the themes and/or lectionary selections of various seasons in the liturgical year. It is my hope that they will enrich your worship on some important holiday occasions.

Most of the readings involve a number of speakers to encourage more participation by lay people in the service. Many were first used as short devotional moments at the start of various meetings and conferences. Some have been used in place of a sermon during less formal summer worship services. These pieces also lend themselves to personal reading and reflection, but my suggestion is, even when reading them alone, to read them aloud. They were written as oral expressions. I have no doubt that you will be creative in finding ways and settings in which to put these readings to work. If you have suggestions or any creative ideas for their use, please write and tell me.

The overall theme of almost all the readings is human transformation and God's ability to create in us a new spirit and a new heart. I believe that the desire for transformation is at the heart of every worship experience. I have tried here to find fresh ways of reading old texts, occasionally even using some slightly irreverent approaches to familiar stories from Scripture. I hope these new approaches will awaken some of the power these texts have to affect people deeply and change their lives. God is speaking to us afresh every day and every time we gather for worship. May some of these readings be among the ways God finds to speak to you or to your congregation.

Advent

John the Baptist,
the Voice of One Crying in the Wilderness

READER

In those days John the Baptist appeared in the wilderness of Judea, proclaiming, "Repent, for the reign of heaven has come near." (Matthew 3:1–2)

RESPONSE

The wilderness was where he belonged, this wild man whose preaching was like the screech of fingernails across a blackboard. Imagine a voice, high and shrill in the gloaming light, reaching out beyond the terrified throng and trying to disturb even the desolated, craggy hills in the distance. Imagine a voice rumbling like an earthquake of the soul, slowly trembling its way into each of those awestruck listeners with one hair-raising word: "Repent!"

Imagine the presence of a spirit as immense and forbidding as the wilderness itself, hundreds of startled faces sneaking looks at it for fear the spirit might look back and burn something, anything into their tentative lives. Imagine the arrival of the reign of heaven declared by this presence so imposing, so savage, that the world did indeed seemed to hang from a thread over a precipice of God's wrath, awaiting God's next sigh. Imagine this drama of one voice so compelling that all the wilderness seemed tame and docile in its presence. Imagine a voice filled with God.

READER

Now John wore clothing of camel's hair with a leather belt around his waist, and his food was locusts and wild honey.

(Matthew 3:4)

RESPONSE

Our John was a Bohemian Baptist, with counterculture clothing and a taste for the bizarre. He allowed no conventional behavior or customary habits to undermine his madman myth. He looked the part of someone playing a part never played before. No priest, no prophet, no sage, no guru had ever stridden through this scene previously. John was unique. Fit to cut a new swath. Poised to open a new door; an oddball of faith to announce the oddest faith of all. Our wild and unpredictable God lays a hand on this weird character; and a miracle of grace will come through ill-fitting camel-hair garb. The holy words will enter our minds on locust breath. And nothing of this faith will ever be conventional again.

READER

Then the people of Jerusalem and all Judea were going out to him, and all the region along the Jordan, and they were baptized by him in the river Jordan, confessing their sins.

(Matthew 3:5–6)

RESPONSE

What drew these crowds, city people with little taste for wild river banks and even wilder ideas? Boredom maybe, or the excitement, or the lure of some fashionable new trend; an adventure down by the holy river, with a spectacle that "you've just got to see." Or maybe, for some, this Baptist was an alarm set to awaken long-drowsy lives, a tremor of life shaking souls long given up for dead. Maybe for some, there were empty places of heart that just needed to be touched, even if it took the scary death grip of a madman in the wilderness.

Then he baptized them. Stunned like deer in the headlights of his stare, these hoping, dreading, longing, aching, trembling people waded down into that muddy water, felt the clutch of John's fanatical hands taking control of everything, spilled their guilty sins into the current and waited for the plunge of faith, for the bath of grace, for a drowning of old lives and old fears in water made holy by their tears and John's insistence. Either yielding or struggling under his fierce grasp, they each must have wondered there in that watery limbo, that little death, that womb of a river, what new life would feel like; what God's new reign in them would mean. Emerging, clean from the muddy flow, spitting and blinking back the dripping of grace, did they see a new day and a grin on that face that shone with God, or were their sins and old habits just waiting for them on the shore?

READER

But when he saw many Pharisees and Sadducees coming for baptism, he said to them, "You brood of vipers! Who warned you to flee from the wrath to come? Bear fruit worthy of repentance. . . . Even now the ax is lying at the root of the trees; every tree therefore that does not bear good fruit is cut down and thrown into the fire." (Matthew 3:7–8, 10)

RESPONSE

Our John was an enraged Baptist. He looked at the world and the superficial parade of posing pilgrims singing "Down by the Riverside" and saw the corruptions of class, and saw the silliness of pretension, and saw the hypocrisy of feigned faith, and saw how joyless was the earnest emptiness. Like the prophet he was, he saw with the eyes of God. He saw beneath the surface of the adoring and complying demeanors, into the souls that no dunking could wash clean and no immersion could transform. A man of wrath, John preached a God of wrath. Injustice raised his ire. His faith was in a God whose furor was an infinite version of his own. John preached fire—grace was not his sermon text, compassion not his theme. God knows, the vipers had it coming, as they always do, but John, in his frenzy, never imagined the most amazing thing of all, that God loved the scoundrels anyway, bad fruit and all.

"I baptize you with water for repentance, but one who is more powerful than I is coming after me; I am not worthy to carry his sandals. He will baptize you with the Holy Spirit and fire."

(*Matthew 3:11*)

Response

When all was said and finished, all of the rage roared, all of the dunking done, all of the wild seething seethed and fuming fumed, John the Baptist told them that he was just the warm-up act. Without even knowing what he meant, he pointed to the next scene in God's drama of transformation: "There is one who is coming who is more powerful than I." In the end, this John and his baptism were just setting the stage for what he could never have imagined: not more wrath, but more grace; not a bigger or more booming presence, but a sadder and wiser lover of the human soul; not an act of power, but a gesture of caring devotion.

John tried to pave the way, clear the decks, make the rough places plain, but nothing he could ever do could prepare this sin-scarred world, this faltering human race, for a gift of such grace as our God of grace had in store. John waited, John believed, John hoped, but the Savior who came must have left him as stunned, startled, and bewildered as he leaves each of us, even here, even now.

––––––

Promises, Promises

"Truly I tell you, there are some standing here who will not taste death before they see the Human One coming in power and glory." (*Matthew 16:28*)

I

We live with words of promise.
Promises, promises, promises.

Swords will be beaten into plowshares.
The meek shall inherit the earth.
The lion and the lamb will share a pillow.
Christ will come again riding on a cloud to
    make everything turn out right.
Those who hunger and thirst for righteousness
    will be filled.

They seem so far away, these pie in the sky promises.
Generations come and go.
Humanity groans and aches.
Hatred and love wax and wane.
People hurt. People starve.
Children are beaten. Leaders lie.
Cities smolder. Crack kills.
Lives hang broken in a breeze of indifference.

And in the midst of it all,
    the words of promise hover there, just out of reach;
    to be seen, heard,
    to tantalize, tease.

But never is the promise fulfilled,
    never does the moment arrive,
    never does God satisfy the thirst for justice,
    never is the hunger for righteousness
    met with that promised feast.
How can we hang our hope, our faith, our lives
    on those hovering, out-of-reach promises?

How can we stake the whole load of this life
    on a ship that never comes in?
How can we live toward a hope that never finds its moment,
    dreaming over and over a dream that never comes true?

A life that dares to listen to the promises
    ends up living the aches, tortured by the longings,
    heaving the sighs too deep for words.

God of promises,
    how long are we supposed to wait?
    how long are we supposed to believe
        in the coming of what never comes?
    how long before an unfilled hope
        becomes nothing but a lie?
    how long before the promise shrivels
        in the face of the pain?
Damn it, God of promises,
    how long?

II

But somehow, we just can't shake it off.
We can't unlearn hope,
    even when it begins to seem futile.
We can't quite stop dreaming
    the dreams that make our souls quiver.
We can't turn off the visions
    that have become part of our seeing,
        even when we just want to close our eyes.

No matter how improbable,
    the future has to be about justice.
We don't know why, but it must.
No matter how unlikely,
    the future has to be about peace.
We don't care what seems realistic,
    or honest or practical, it simply must.
No matter how ridiculous it may seem,
    the future has to be about liberation,
        and sharing,
        and finding some kind of love
        at the heart of it all.

It just has to.
We don't know how else to live.

The future is about the presence of God.
We believe it because that's the promise,
And you, impossible, unlikely,
    improbable, unexpected God,
    you keep promises.
You keep promises.
You keep promises.

Four Readings on the Themes of Advent

HOPE

*May the God of hope fill you with all joy and peace in
believing, so that you may abound in hope by the power of
the Holy Spirit.*   (*Romans 15:13*)

Advent is about hope. George Herbert once wrote: "He that believes in hope dances without music." It is an apt metaphor for a
life of faith. To hope in God's grace is to move to a rhythm un-
heard by others, to act out a drama unfathomed by those around
you, to glide through life guided by a tune playing only in your
own heart. God knows, the hopes of our faith make no sense
from the outside. In a world where corruption and power domi-
nate and control our lives, we hope that a God of truth and justice will have the final word. In a world where violence and force
of arms always seem to win the day, we hope that a force of love
is the ultimate power. In a world where wealth and position sit
astride desperately oppressed populations, we hope that poverty
and innocence have God's special blessing. To have such hope
means to constantly expect a different kind of a future, even as
day after day slides into a history that confirms our most cynical

fears. To have such hope means to act as if God's presence were moving through every moment of life, even when God seems distant as the moon.

Shakespeare wrote: "The miserable have no other medicine, but only hope." Hope is for those who feel the ache of the world. Hope is for those who agonize at human cruelty; for those made miserable by the sight of homeless children; for those who hear the cries of refugees and cry along with them. Hope is for those whose souls can find no other balm. In a world under a shadow of violence and injustice, we sing, "Watcher, tell us of the night, what its signs of promise are." We are those who listen for the voice of angels on the wind; who stretch to see the first light of a new day on the horizon; who long for a new birth of grace in every human heart. We wait. We listen. We hope.

PEACE

And the peace of God, which surpasses all understanding,
will guard your hearts and your minds in Christ Jesus.
(Philippians 4:7)

Advent is about peace. And we do so long for peace. We live in a world of chaos and discord. The trademark of our times is violence, but it has always been thus. In a nation awash in guns, we continue to raise our children on myths of machismo. Our movie heroes are still tough-talking, gun-wielding musclemen. Our streets are dangerous. Our civil dialogue has given way to abusive rhetoric. And a routine trip through a busy intersection is often enough to give us a glimpse of at least one other driver's middle finger. In it all, we do so long for peace.

The state of our minds mirrors the state of our world. We juggle hyperactive schedules, fragmented families, and hypertensive pressures. We worry about our children, we agonize over how to care for our parents, and no job seems safe. Our choices of antacid are outnumbered only by our spiritual options. We grasp for gurus and scan self-help books in serial confusion. Stress is the name of our days. And we do so long for peace.

Surely the peace of the world starts with the peace of a heart. We are reminded that there is a peace of God which passes all understanding. At the core of each of us, if we but listen, there is a still, small voice which can calm our fears, quiet our lives, and dispel our desperation. At the heart of each of us, if we but seek it, there is a spirit that rests in the grace of God. An assurance at the center of our lives can tame the chaos at the edges. That spirit of God is also the hope of our world. Peace can come only when we can understand each other, knowing that God's spirit makes us truly one. In the eyes of even a murderer, I can see my own anger. In the face of a terrorist, I can see my own desperation. In the breast of my enemy, I can feel my own fear. Peace is possible because we share that one spirit that rests in the presence of God. Not one of us is stranger to another. Every passion or malice that might separate us I can find and recognize in my own heart, and so our differences lose their force. We are one with each other, and one with God, and that is a peace beyond the power of any stress or violence that can assault us. As we await our Bringer of Peace, the peace of God is already with us.

JOY

Rejoice in the Sovereign always; again I will say, Rejoice.
(*Philippians* 4:4)

Advent is about joy. But our times seem little suited for rejoicing. Our culture irritates and titillates, entertains and intoxicates, excites and numbs, but rejoicing seems a foreign notion. One can't rejoice on cue. Joy cannot be purchased or peddled. You can't plan for it or train for it. It doesn't fit into a well-ordered life and is not FDA approved. Joy comes only when least expected. We rejoice only when life has been turned on its ear; when, whatever we feared, whatever we steeled ourselves against, some gift of God has presented itself instead. When we rein in our loves to protect ourselves from pain, when we curtail our hopes from fear of disillusionment, when we equip ourselves with cynicism to avoid looking the fool, we do so at the expense of joy.

As freedom can only be tasted in all its sweetness by those who know the feel of chains, so joy sings with its most full-throated glory only in spirits enlarged by the weight of despair and softened by the brine of tears. Pleasures float on the surface of life.

Happiness flits across a moment or an hour. But joy springs from the depths. Joy is new life beating in a heart that has been broken. Joy is awakening to a fair morning from a nightmare of reality. Joy is a flight sunward on wings you had forgotten you had. Joy is the sound of laughter erupting from a cortege of grief. Joy is God's melody amid the discord of life, a song carrying the lilt of eternity and touching the chords of longing in our souls.

LOVE

And this is my prayer, that your love may overflow more and more with knowledge and full insight. (*Philippians* 1:9)

Advent is about love. Francis Bacon once wrote: "A crowd is not company, faces are but a gallery of pictures, and talk but a tinkling cymbal, where there is no love." We are social beings. That is our blessing and our curse. We long for each other. We long to touch, to share, to bare some part of ourselves, to be understood, to invite others into our lives. We all long to assuage the loneliness that lurks in the background of even our most crowded moments. We are born alone and we will ultimately die alone, but in between we desperately want to be known, to be understood, to belong, to find some unqualified acceptance, some intimacy of soul. And so we reach out with fragile, tenuous efforts of love.

But love is dangerous. We hurt each other. When you choose to care about another, you can get your heart broken. If you reach out, you can be rejected, and that is more painful than never reaching out at all. If you try to belong, to give yourself to some group, you can be excluded, and that hurts more deeply even than being alone. Love, and the attendant risks of being open, exposed, and vulnerable, spawns ugly jealousies, irrational fears, and painful misunderstandings. There is no love without such risks. Love scares us to death. But like hunger and thirst, the longing for love is implanted in our deepest selves. God strews our paths with opportunities to care and people whose own needs clutch at our own.

There is some part of this gift of life that does not keep, that can't be stored up or locked away. Some part of this spirit that God has placed within us dies if we do not spend it or share it or give it away.

Love is always a risk, but it is a risk upon which the very heart of our life depends. To love is to touch the heart of God. To look into the eyes of another and recognize our common soul is to see the face of God. Even to feel the ache of a heart broken for love is to discover God's grace. As Tasso wrote: "Any time that is not spent on love is wasted."

———

From Bethlehem
(Based on prophecies from Micah)

✧

READER

But you, O Bethlehem of Ephrathah, who are one of the little clans of Judah, from you shall come forth for me one who is to rule in Israel, whose origin is from of old, from ancient days. (Micah 5:2)

RESPONSE

From the littlest comes one who shall be great.
From the forgotten people
    comes one we can never forget.
From the overlooked comes one
    who reaches into our lives and cannot be overlooked.
From the ordinary
    comes an explosion of the extraordinary.
Where we do not, cannot, will not, dare not,
    expect you, God,
You come and dwell among us.

READER

Therefore he shall give them up until the time when she who is in travail has brought forth; then the rest of his kindred shall return to the people of Israel. (Micah 5:3)

RESPONSE

She who is in travail shall bring forth.

Travail is the name of our times, God.
Our arrogance hides our inner agony.
   We are in travail.
Our greedy consumption hides our inner emptiness and despair.
   We are in travail.
Our tough competition hides our childish fears.
   We are in travail.

In these days of labor and stress,
   of worry and pain,
   of gathering gloom,
   in these days of travail,
We wait to bring forth . . . something.

To bring forth some moment of grace,
   some birth of hope,
   some light of truth,
   some spirit of healing.
In our travail, we are waiting to bring forth.

READER
*And the ruler shall stand and feed the flock in the strength
of the Sovereign, in the majesty of the name of the Sovereign. And they shall live secure, for now the ruler shall be
great to the ends of the earth.* (Micah 5:4)

RESPONSE
We hunger for righteousness, and he shall feed us.
We hunger for justice, and he shall feed us.
We hunger for love,
   and he shall feed his flock.
We who know and see and fear
   all the weakness that is at the heart of us,
   especially in our strength and power,
   shall find his strength,
Your strength, O God.

And we who worry
   and feel the hopes and fears of all the years,
We will dwell secure.
We who have made insecurity into a way of life,
      hiding from truth,
      stockpiling masses of desolate might,
Finally, we will dwell secure,
For you shall be great.

READER
And the ruler shall be the one of peace. (Micah 5:5a)

RESPONSE
And this shall be peace.
Yes, God, you have spoken, you have promised.
And this shall be peace.

Christmas

Hearing the Story Again

We've come together tonight to hear again that old story of a stable, and a baby born to a peasant couple, alone and far from home. It's a story that we've heard every year for as long as we can remember. We know it as well as we know our own past. We have images from a hundred pictures, from our own imaginations at every age: images of what the stable was like, of Mary's face and how she held the baby, of how the Magi looked and how many shepherds came; images of cows and sheep and the donkey.

This story is so wrapped up in our own Christmases past that it has become a part of us. It is our history now too. We have had years of singing it, imagining it, reading it, seeing it acted out by generations of children; celebrating it. These things have made it our story.

But this story is something beyond our own personal past. We know it is a story that has been part of the lives of generation after generation of people—listening to it and reliving it across twenty centuries. It is a story that connects us tonight with the lives of those hundred generations who have sat year after year, just as we do now, hearing it and making it their own.

There is a power here in what we do tonight. It is the power of eternity touching a moment of time. It is the power of God becoming real for us again. So let us listen and let this tale work its magic in us once more.

The Journey

‹※›

The story starts with the decision of an emperor to conduct a census. Maybe it was a good imperial decision that would benefit the empire. Maybe it was a whim. Maybe it was a bureaucratic boondoggle. But whatever it was, it was a simple thing for the emperor. One day the great Augustus made up his mind, signed a few orders, put some bureaucrat in charge, then went off to lunch.

But as is so often the case when the powerful make even a minor decision, the powerless everywhere had their lives changed. Two thousand miles away, peasant families paid a price for the emperor's little decision. A betrothed couple in a little town called Nazareth, a town the emperor had never heard of, was one of these.

A young woman, almost still a girl, after facing the disgrace of a pregnancy out of wedlock, leaves home for probably the very first time, on a journey. An older man, a struggling tradesman, betrothed to a woman about to give birth to a child that is not his, leaves home on this same journey even though he can't afford the expense or the time. It is a trip taken at the wrong time. She is nearing the time of labor. It is winter. The ground is hard. The wind is biting cold. It is a long trip for poor people who have to walk most of the way. They are alone. There is no one to help or comfort strangers on the road. There is nothing to stop the pangs of labor when they come. It is a trip taken at the wrong time.

And so on a cold night, a hundred miles from home, they come into a town that is not very hospitable to strangers from far-off places, in a world not very hospitable to poor and homeless people. They come to Bethlehem.

The Shepherds

‹※›

Those impetuous shepherds, picture them, dancing off across the fields like crazy drunks, to the rhythm of a music no one else could hear. But they were only drunk on the spirit and the magic of a starlit winter night. Who knows what they saw or what they thought they heard that night? Who knows what voices sang of wonder and wisdom in their ears? But we do know that they responded, cavorting down the hillsides with their feet hardly touching the ground, until, out of breath, almost exhausted, they stumbled upon a miracle.

Only those few shepherds were there for the birth of a light that banishes the shadows, for the coming of a new kind of leader. Everyone else in town slept through it or never noticed. The rest of the world just went about its business. They never heard any angels. They never felt any magic. But the shepherds were ready for a miracle. The shepherds were waiting and watching and willing to follow. We too must ready ourselves for wonder. We must open our minds for mystery. We must widen our eyes for awe and clear our ears for the music of God's world. Miracles await those with watchful hearts.

The Angels

In our rational, hardheaded world, it's hard to imagine a sky full of angels. How many of us have heard the beating of angels' wings or heard their song high and wild on a starlit night? How often have we been touched by the magic of things unseen and mysteries that lie just over the threshold of belief?

Maybe more than we think. Maybe those angels have been there often, but our memories are dim and our perceptions are weak. Maybe something has buoyed us up when hopelessness had us in its grip. Maybe there have been times when some barely noticed tap on the shoulder has awakened us to a moment of beauty or a miracle of life. Maybe there have been times when some hidden nudge has sent us left rather than right, and that has made all the difference.

Or maybe the angels of our time are not so subtle at all. Maybe we are angels to each other. The friend who held your hand during the longest night of your life, the stranger whose smile was timed just right to redeem a bad day, the acquaintance whose hug gave you a welcome when you felt left out; maybe angels are all around us. Maybe the heavens open every day; whenever love touches a moment, wherever grace breaks through, whatever comes to us unearned, undeserved, and makes our lives richer and more wonderful.

Listen and you'll hear them, voices high and wild in the night. Watch and you'll see them, angels, forever taking us unawares and telling us of the miracles in our midst.

———

The Birth

Those startled shepherds walk bedazzled across the fields at night to find a miracle. What they find is an ordinary baby. King Herod trembles in his palace at the thought of a rival. What he's afraid of is just an ordinary baby. Three Magi travel a thousand miles to witness a cosmic event. What they see is an ordinary baby; the wrinkled skin, the cute little fingers and toes, the little arms and legs pushing and pulling at the air in a dance of discovery, the crying, the cuddling, the new moment of life.

But perhaps no baby is ordinary at all. Birth calls forth new love from all those who see it. It reawakens our awe at the miracle of life. And in every baby there is potential for far beyond anything we can guess or imagine. This baby would change the world. This birth has continued to touch all of humanity ever since.

This birth can happen to us tonight. It is the birth of a child whose name is love in each of our wounded hearts. It is the birth of a child whose name is grace in each of our broken lives. It is the birth of a child whose name is warmth in every cold corner of our being. You have but to give yourself to this magical birth and your own soul will flutter like angels' wings. Your own imagination will shine like the brightest of stars. Your own mind will tremble like an awestruck shepherd. Your own life will pour forth new gifts like a wandering king at a manger.

———

The Star

⚜

The Magi walked in the light of a sky lit by a single star. Radiant beyond any other, that star drew them across hundreds of uncharted miles and through dozens of strange cities. Who knows how these sages managed to follow a star. Who knows what they thought they would find, or what they thought they would do when they found it. But don't we all follow stars in our lives? Don't we chase after dreams, even if they are a little vague or unlikely, hoping and wishing that they might come true? Don't we all chase after our own secret notions of what we're meant to be, at least half believing that some fate has our lives in its grasp? Don't we all long for some special miracle in our lives; the knight in shining armor, the beautiful sleeping princess, the pot of gold at the end of the rainbow, the living happily ever after?

Somewhere in our souls or spirits or hearts, God has placed a star for us to follow. It's a star called longing, a star called faith. We long for a truth to live for, and we believe that there really is one. We long for something that will give peace to the places where we ache and agonize, and we believe there is such a peace. We long for a sign that love is stronger than hatred in the world, and we believe in our God of love. We long for some place to bow down and give our gifts, and we believe there is such a place. And so we are seekers. We are star followers. We are pilgrims; journeyers of faith; wrestlers with doubts; seekers after truth; travelers on a road of uncertain destination. We have no map. We have no directions. We have no guide. We have only a star that God has placed in our souls; and a call to follow.

But the promise is that there are miracles to discover. There is the very presence of God to touch us. There is a new birth waiting out there that can change all our lives.

What Difference Does It Make?

✣

I

At some point, the celebration ends, the visits and the parties are over, and things get back to the way things are. Normal, ordinary, routine. We've had our refreshing little dose of giving and receiving gifts, of sentiment and warmth. Maybe we have reconnected with family or cried over the lack of family in our lives. Maybe we've had a time of memories and good cheer or made a pilgrimage to the church of our choice.

Maybe that's all the season and the holiday amounts to, and maybe that's enough. We need this kind of stuff once a year. We need some measure of warm sentiments. We need a reason to reconnect with family and old friends. We need to discover again that it can feel good to give gifts to each other. Maybe, all of this is enough.

II

But didn't we want it to mean so much more? Didn't we celebrate this event that makes all the difference and changes everything that is? Aren't we those who believe that this Christ child redeems the world? But how? Is it different? Can we look around this world objectively, dispassionately, and really say that the birth of Christ changes things? Can we really say that our cozy and sentimental celebrations of Christmas have made any long-standing difference at all, once the world has gotten back to what we call normal? If this is a redeemed world, where do we see that redemption, where do we point to the difference? Has the killing stopped? Has the greed lost its grip? Have the powerful suddenly grown attentive to the needs of the poor? If we are saved but can't tell the difference, what does salvation mean?

III

We have shared, yet again, the Christmas message that Christ is born, that God is revealed and present in a human birth and a human child; that God is alive in the ordinary humanness of simple people in poor circumstances. If you think it is just part of a nice story or some romantic myth from another age, if you think it is a child's fairy tale that you listen to once a year like you might listen to

Cinderella, then it doesn't make any difference. Your world is untouched. You've had your holiday. Kiss your mother and your aunt Martha and go back to work. Christmas is an agreeable celebration and then it's over. The world is the same. You are the same. You've had your refreshing time and now your life goes on.

IV

But if you believe that this Christmas story has told us, anew, something fundamental about the way life is and the way we are and God is; if you believe that this Christmas story is your story about where the meaning is and where the forgiveness is and where the love is in your life and my life and the life of this whole planet; if you really believe that, then nothing is the same. Nothing can ever be the same. When you have once again celebrated this Christmas mystery, the celebration doesn't just go away. It is not over. The reawakening of love has made you a new person. No sharing of love is ever without its transforming effect on the heart.

It is because our lives have been touched by this birth of love that we live and give and care as we do. It is because our lives are grasped by the spirit of Christ that we get up in the morning and hug our kids and do our best and want to sing now and then. It is because we are in love with this vision of life that we have hope, no matter what, and a reason to be and laugh and reach out. It makes all the difference because this celebration was just a reminder to keep our eyes open to the God around us and the Christ beside us and the Spirit that is in us.

Epiphany

The Magi

Our imaginations have always been drawn to this trio. It must have been a sight, strange even then. We picture them on camels, three grand figures moving across the landscape in colorful robes and the kind of strange hats fit only for Magi. Old and learned, yet open to miracles and the voices of prophecy from a faith not their own, they are the archetypal pilgrims. They follow signs in the heavens. They read the ancient books. They understand mysteries and magical powers. They arrange their lives around omens and portents. And so they find this tiny miracle in a stable that everyone else has missed.

Perhaps we find these strange figures appealing because they have given their lives to some sort of quest. They are seekers. They follow stars and look for the meanings behind our everyday reality. We can imagine in them that romantic joie de vivre that seems so lacking in the tediousness of our everyday lives. The pilgrim seeker in us wants some journey of faith as compelling as theirs. We hunger for the courage to follow and pursue our own dreams. We long for a time when we are not so tied down to responsibilities and duties and making a living, so that we too can go after the elusive meaning of it all. As we skim the surface of life, we too want to plunge into that journey of discovery to uncover the secrets and ponder the heart of faith. These wise travelers are the pilgrim soul in all of us, gazing at stars and decoding ancient wisdom.

They must have had a hard trek. There must have been many dangers on the road for wealthy foreigners. One imagines them traveling at night under the stars, but one seldom imagines the rain, the cold, the hard ground, the suspicious locals, the expense of the expedition, the risks of making such a journey. How did they manage to make such a commitment on such meager evidence, such an unknown outcome? And in the end, the treachery of Herod makes them players in a more devilish drama. Even for them, there is the chance that their wisdom and dedication will be used for a more cynical and sinister purpose.

We understand the hardships. Everything we set out to accomplish seems more complicated and more arduous than we expected. We wish we had the boldness to pursue the life we long for with such dedication and perseverance, with so little encouragement to go on. But most of us want to be sure before we throw our life into something. Most of us can't manage to take the leap and risk so much for just a dream or just a chance. How often do our fears keep us from those nighttime roads of faith? How often do we fail to seize a moment or chase a hope because we fear failure or won't risk the cost of humiliation or disappointment? And along the way, of course, we are also apt to sell our dreams to the powers that be. We serve so many little Herods who use us and our labor for ends we don't even want to contemplate. We are so easily seduced by the flattery of being valuable or useful to those whose wealth or prestige or celebrity impresses us. Our mystical Magi longings are so trapped in the petty anxieties of our daily living.

Reader 3

But what does this trek of the Magi really mean? What are they after? They go to give their gifts, of course. They go to bow down before something that transcends their magic and reaches beyond the grasp of their lore. They are seeking some wisdom beyond everything that is wise, some truth that still eludes their spiritual study. They are looking for that most elusive yet transparent of mysteries. They are seeking God.

At heart, perhaps, that is the only thing worth seeking for any of us. We all need to worship, to give the gift of our lives, our time, our commitment, our hearts to something worthy of such a gift. We all want to bow down before something that makes sense of the chaos and cruelty and injustice around us. We all need to feel that, no matter how well or badly our lives turn out, we matter for something in the ultimate scheme of things. Yes, we desperately want there to be some ultimate scheme of things. So we seek, we wonder, and we hope. On this journey of life, we can only bow down, as this enigmatic trio did so long ago, and trust that God receives our gift.

The Baptism of Jesus

In those days Jesus came from Nazareth of Galilee and was baptized by John in the Jordan. And just as he was coming up out of the water, he saw the heavens torn apart and the Spirit descending like a dove on him. And a voice came from heaven, "You are my Child, the Beloved; with you I am well pleased." (Mark 1:9–11)

Every life of faith begins with the experience of God. Maybe responding to some potent words from that wild wilderness prophet, John, or maybe just following the lead of his own restless spirit, Jesus decides to be baptized in the holy river Jordan. He stands there, chest deep in the current, waiting for that symbolic plunge. Was some prayer running through his mind? Some misgiving or hesitation? Did he expect an epiphany or hope for a heavenly voice? Or did he just look at that overpowering Baptist and give himself up to the moment? With little ceremony, he was suddenly dunked into the muddy water. That little death, that washing away of guilt, that drowning of past life probably didn't feel symbolic at all. One womblike moment of limbo in the grasp of powerful hands, feeling a little out of control, and then he is back in the brightness of a midday sun, a trickle of water running down his face, the gasp of a breath of air feeling like his very first breath. And then it happened.

There is nothing but metaphor to describe it; nothing but the blunt instrument of ancient words now worn out by repetition. But

God touched him there, as he stood dripping in the stream. Maybe the heavens of his soul split open and a godlike voice boomed into his consciousness. Maybe he was overwhelmed by the joy of a holy moment and a still, small voice echoed somewhere in his mind. Or maybe his heart broke at the glory of seeing that sun-splashed day like the newborn that he was and a bird song sounded like an angel choir. Choose your own metaphor of theophany, they all mean the same thing. The God of all eternity, blossomed into a moment of time. The God of all creation, poured forth into the spirit of one human being. The God of the whole of the cosmos, erupted into one person's wide-open life. And that moment; that descending dove of spirit; that rising birth of God's love in him, started it all. All of his passion, all of his wisdom, all of his courage, that unconquerable fire of justice, that unquenchable warmth of love, all grew out of that moment. For there, rising out of the waters of the Jordan, Jesus gave his soul to God and God created a new heart within him. In that moment he knew that he was God's child.

To follow Christ is to look for, to hope for such moments in our own days and nights. To follow Christ is to try to open our own lives to that touch of God deep within us that can transform every fiber of our living with the power of grace. We too can be reborn as the children of God in any moment when we see the world anew, or recognize God's love in another human face, or hear in an everyday sound that angel choir singing of eternity. That same direct, heaven-splitting experience of God is offered to us as well.

Fishermen with a Call

⚜

READER

Jesus came to Galilee, proclaiming the good news of God, and saying, "The time is fulfilled, and the reign of God has come near; repent, and believe in the good news."

As Jesus passed along the Sea of Galilee, he saw Simon and his brother Andrew casting a net into the sea—for they were fishermen. And Jesus said to them, "Follow me and I will make you fish for people." (Mark 1:14b–17)

RESPONSE

Why in the world was it fishermen he chose?

Casting nets is hardly a qualification for a journey of faith.
They met no ministerial guidelines,
Had no clinical training,
No advanced degrees in discipleship.
They couldn't even catch fish all that well.

For the awe-filled job of changing the world,
    of staring down the powers of death,
    of forging new ways of thinking and living and loving;
For the grandest task there could ever be,
Jesus just walked down to the lake
    and called to a bunch of fishermen.

Absurd idea.

He called out to the ordinary folks,
    to the plain people,
    to a bunch of guys who wouldn't know a theology from a fish story.

No expertise,
No brilliant minds or exciting talents,
No ordinations or installations,
Just a call.

Just a call like yours and mine and ours.

READER

And immediately they left their nets and followed him. As he
went a little farther, he saw James son of Zebedee and his
brother John, who were in their boat mending the nets. Imme-
diately he called them; and they left their father Zebedee in the
boat with the hired men, and followed him.

(Mark 1:18–20)

Response

And why in the world did they go with him?
An odd-looking stranger walks down the beach.
He says, "Follow me!"
And they drop their nets,
    they drop their father,
    they drop their work,
    they drop their lives and their homes.
With not a word to each other
    they just follow the odd stranger.

Are they deranged?
    Do they misunderstand?
    Are they fleeing some "quiet desperation"?
Or are they just chasing after any chance at life that doesn't smell
    of fish?
What could they have seen or heard in him?
Was it his eyes that burned with passion or love
    or God (whatever that looks like)?
Was it some godly authority in his voice;
    some basso-profundo command
    that left them quaking in their fishy boots?
Or was it some "still, small" certainty that touched something
    long untouched in their waterlogged souls?

How do you tell the call of a Christ
    from the raving of a crank?

But whatever it was, they were hooked
    like minnows on forty-pound test line.
They walked out of the routine of just getting by,
    of just making a living,
And signed on for a voyage of new life in the making;
Riding the waves of passionate longings and daring fears;
An adventure of bigger-than-life hopes and soul-shaking risks.

They followed a crazy faith,
    a life-or-death dream,
    a hard-to-believe promise,

The light in the eyes of either a lunatic
or an improbable, unimaginable Messiah.

And they came to life
in ways that they didn't even know were possible.

READER
He called to them and they followed him.

Transfiguration

READER 1
On a bright, sun-washed day in midwinter, Jesus took his three
closest friends and set out to climb a mountain. Like Moses and
Elijah before him, at a turning point in his life, he sought the
presence of God on a mountaintop. In the months since John the
Baptist was beheaded, Jesus had been constantly on the move,
delaying the inevitable arrest. And now, beginning to feel that he
had to go to Jerusalem to force a final confrontation, he sought a
time of prayer and silence to seek in his own heart the will of
God.

All morning they climbed the mountain. A steep winding path
led through deep gorges and under cliff faces. It traversed banks
of loose rocks and forced them to crawl hand over hand up the
most precipitous slopes. The hard going released some of the tension that Jesus had been feeling as he thought of his future. The
four men began to laugh and tease each other as they went, something they hadn't done much recently. It was good to face a foe as
simple and concrete as a mountainside. They began to experience again the easy camaraderie they had once enjoyed.

READER 2
As Jesus relaxed, letting go of the pressure of coming to a decision, he began to realize why the decision was so hard. Life was
good, and he loved it. He wasn't ready to walk away from all the
small pleasures that made life so rich. There was the sight and

smell of the campfire at night, and the way the water on the lake rippled as a breeze blew across it. There was the look of love and longing in the eyes of the women who followed him, and the relief and gratitude of those whose lives he touched with simple acts of care. There was the taste of sweet spring water, the smell of sweat in the hot sun, the sound of birds just before the dawn, the touch of another human being. Life was indeed good, and he did not want to become a martyr as John the Baptist had been.

When they reached a level place near the top of the mountain, Jesus left the others to work his way to the top alone. He finally sat down on the edge of a steep drop overlooking the mountainside. He dangled his feet over the edge, took a long draft of water from his goatskin bag, and began to quietly speak aloud. The mystery of prayer for him was just that. He would simply speak his thoughts aloud, rambling and unfocused, and gradually begin to feel that God was emerging in his own mind and words, speaking through his own jumble of thoughts as they worked themselves out.

He ran through all his reservations, spoke aloud of all his options. But when he began to speak of going to Jerusalem his words grew taut and focused, and passion began to enter his voice. He felt the need to challenge the way things were, the law-bound self-righteousness of his own tradition. He didn't want to just slip away quietly or be arrested in some little town of Galilee. For at least one proud moment he wanted to stand at the very center of Jerusalem and speak for those whose voices had never been heard; to shout once with power for those forever without any power. He wanted to stand defiantly at the center of their faith, just once, as a symbol of those who had been pushed forever outside. He would go there and shed a tear that mattered for all of those who felt that they didn't matter.

As he spoke he realized that his voice had grown louder. In his mind, the reservations were fading away. Yes, maybe one grand gesture was worth the ultimate sacrifice. Maybe one enduring act could make a difference, kindle a fire, open a few hearts, start a movement, be a source of hope for those desperately needing hope. He was almost shouting the words now.

READER 1

As the three disciples tried to nap among the rocks, John suddenly awoke, certain he had heard loud voices above him. He woke the others. Thinking something might be amiss, they followed Jesus' path to the top. As they looked up into the glare of the setting sun, they saw him. He was not alone. There seemed to be other figures near him among the rocks. He seemed to be talking to someone. Peter began to speak about Moses and Elijah and miracles and tabernacles. James and John just stood staring as Jesus turned and started walking down toward them.

Maybe it was the sunset. Maybe it was the remnant of sleep in their eyes. But as he approached, there was a glow, a fullness, a certain majesty about him. Gone was the indecisive man who had started up the mountain that morning. He had changed. Something had happened on that mountaintop. They all knew it. They could feel it. Peter, in his bold, bumbling way, blurted out in excitement that it was like Moses when his face was shining after speaking with God. He spoke of Elijah hearing the voice.

Jesus said nothing. He just gazed at them and smiled. A cloud blew across the sunset. Even in the dusk there did seem to be a light in him. And inside each of them, a still, small voice seemed to grow with the assurance that this one human being next to them was filled with a Spirit of God, as no one ever was before or might ever be again.

READER 2

The cloud passed on. Jesus clasped his arm around the shoulders of two of his friends, and in the fading light, they set off on the road that led to Jerusalem. He knew now that it was the right road.

Lent

Returning to God
(Ash Wednesday)

READER

Yet even now, says God, return to me with all your heart, with fasting, with weeping, and with mourning. (Joel 2:12)

This is the season of Lent, we are called to repent.

But how do I return to God? The journey seems beyond what I can manage. My days are dominated by a hundred other gods. Out of fear, I have huddled behind the walls of prejudice. I have narrowed my living until it could flow within the banks of propriety.

I have been a mute witness to cruelty, and have gladly donned the blinders and the masks of my safe little circle of society. Out of greed, I have enslaved myself to a cycle of consuming and accumulation. Out of envy, I have ridiculed the foibles and enjoyed the failures of people I've called friends. Out of emptiness, I have thrown away precious hours, benumbed by that flickering and titillating screen. Out of laziness, I have sunk into a stifling and stultifying status quo.

Yes, I can weep and mourn for the lost soul of my life and ache when I turn my vague and wistful aspirations to God, but can I return? Can I renounce the sin that has become the very routine of my aching days? Yes, I can weep, but God still seems beyond my reach, beyond the moon.

READER

Rend your hearts and not your clothing. (Joel 2:13a)

But our hearts are already rent. When God is just a distant flicker on a far horizon, it is not just about our guilt and our failures of courage and goodness. We are wounded people, our hearts long broken from the struggle. The hurts of lifetimes keep hurting, and we don't let them go.

Sometimes, an old stray memory will sting into my consciousness, reminding me of some long-discarded dream, the grief of some abandoned possibility. Sometimes there are just little things in the course of a day: casual snubs from near strangers, quiet little failures of nerve, ways that we hurt those we love, little letdowns from those we counted on, the precious moments that we let slip by in empty procession. Everything we know is passing away, and every loss tears away a piece of our caring.

God, we have made mistakes and we regret them. And it all builds up, hurts, wounds, disappointments, never-healing scars. We are all broken people, in a thousand little ways and a few big ones. Just as our faces begin to weather and show the wear of our years, so do our hearts and souls get wrinkled and scarred, weathered and gray. Some of it we can blame on others, or on the accidents of life, or on the world's cruelty. But the deepest lines and the scars that disfigure most are our own creations.

Don't tell us to rend our hearts, they are already broken.

READER
Return to the Sovereign, your God, for God is gracious and
merciful, slow to anger, and abounding in steadfast love, and
relents from punishing. (*Joel 2:13b*)

But wherever the brokenness comes from, it is our story. And every now and then, my God, we want that steadfast love that can heal. We long to be grasped by the power of life itself and renewed and made whole. We need the grace of a God who lets us start fresh and live new. We need a mercy that can touch the pieces of our own souls that have withered and died. Let God's love be steadfast and God's graciousness and mercy be beyond all measure, for only then can our cowering spirits be loved out of their hiding places and our battered hearts be graced from their sickness. We have not the courage or the folly to return to God as we are, and yet God's love draws us and leads us and cajoles us and humors us into trust. That steadfast love is our only hope, but it is hope indeed.

In the wilderness of our living, we are loved. Knowing that, maybe even such as we can return to that bosom of grace and that fountain of mercy that is our God.

This is the season of Lent, we are called to repent.

The Wilderness

✤

READER

And the Spirit immediately drove him out into the wilderness.
He was in the wilderness forty days, tempted by Satan; and he
was with the wild beasts; and the angels waited on him.

(Mark 1:12–13)

VOICE 1

I know the wilderness. I've been there too.
I've been there in hours and days of grief.
I've grieved for lives swallowed by death:
    some deaths that have only echoed through my life
    with the sound of long-closed doors locking forever;
    but also those deaths that have ripped open gashes in my heart
        and mind,
    that have left gaping holes in my life.
I've also known that wilderness of grief over words of love
    that I was too afraid to say;
Over parts of my self that have died from disuse;
Over dear friends who have drifted
    out of my life and will never be found again.

I've been there in that comfortless desert that echoes with the grief of all people.
No shelter there from the tears.
No shade there from the pain.
No place to hide there from the emptiness inside.
The wilderness is life.

VOICE 2

I know the wilderness. I too have been there.
I've been there at times when I've had no hope.
> Sometimes it's been personal. Up against a wall of failure,
> with no one left to blame and nothing to hide my inadequacy;
> or under a landslide of guilt, feeling dirty and twisted and
> > without worth.
Without that fragile hint of hope, life is a wilderness.

But sometimes it's bigger than I am.
Just reading the newspaper can bring on a despair for the whole
> weeping planet.
> > Hatred and violence breed in poverty and injustice,
> > infecting new generations as the old one passes
> > > decimated into twilight.
Where is the hope when children of starvation compete for headlines
> with children of abuse and neglect, where understanding seems rare
> and prejudice is the rule.

I've been there in the wilderness,
Where there's no shelter from despair;
Where there's no shade from the glare of guilt;
Where there's no place to hide from ourselves.
The wilderness is the human race.

VOICE 3

I know this lonely and desolate wilderness. I've been there.
I've been there because I've built walls around my life to keep
> others out:
> > Walls of fear, because I've been hurt;
> > Walls of aggression, because sometimes I want to hurt back.
I am afraid of people and what they might think of me;
> how they might judge. I'd rather judge them first.
I reach out, but it's a fleeting thing, I pull back
> before anyone can even think of rejecting me.
Locked within the prison of this well-defended life,
> this well-fortified self,

I know this wilderness where the only sound
  is my own voice protesting the emptiness.
The wilderness is me.

VOICE 4
You have a companion in that wilderness; someone who wanders
    there with you.
The grief, the hopelessness, the loneliness, are not yours alone.

Somewhere in that wilderness, there is God.
Somewhere, beyond all hope of shelter,
  God is a roof from the storm.
Somehow, beyond all imagining of shade,
  God is an overarching tree.
Some way, in the most terrifying moment of silence,
  God is a voice that touches you where you ache for touch.
Somewhere, when you've forgotten how to get out of that
    wilderness,
  God will be there, calling you out and leading the way.

I know, because I've been there too.
I've wandered that wilderness with the rest of you,
  and at the end of my strength, the angels came and ministered
    to me.
And God led me out of that wilderness to change the world.

––––––––

Loose Living: The Prodigal Son

✦

READER
*Then Jesus said, "There was a man who had two sons. The
younger of them said to his father, 'Father, give me the share of
the property that will belong to me.' So he divided his property
between them. A few days later the younger son gathered all he
had and traveled to a distant country, and there he squandered
his property in dissolute living."* (*Luke 15:11–13*)

RESPONSE 1

We know this lad. He wants to grab what he's entitled to and set out on his own. Papa's rules are no longer for him. He wants his own way, his own life, his own world. Freedom, independence, autonomy, individualism, these are his gods; and a far country is where he wants to worship them. Far away from responsibilities, away from guilts or duties, away from the people who might frown or disapprove because they know that he should be better or do better or care more, that's where he wants to be.

Dissolute living is what he wants to pursue. He has that lust to indulge himself, to chase his fantasies and cross the boundaries, and to take off the straitjacket of family and expectations. Maybe he doesn't want to be what he was raised to be, what he was carefully, parentally prepared to become. He must find his own life, his own tastes, his own rules, and how can he find out who he is if he doesn't explore and experiment and reach for that great unknown romance of experience and exploits?

RESPONSE 2

Yes, we know this young person, all rebellion and self-absorption, because we are him. Most of us, too, reject the handed-down wisdom of traditions to seek some way of life we can label our own. Even if we never seek that far-off country, there are times when we long for it; for ways to avoid the omniscient gaze of the ones we call father and mother. We too have thrown away or mis-used so many of the gifts we have inherited. We too know what it is to turn our backs on what we know is right, or what we've been told is our duty. Our living is often a little dissolute.

READER

"When he had spent everything, a severe famine took place throughout that country, and he began to be in need. So he went and hired himself out to one of the citizens of that country, who sent him to his fields to feed the pigs. He would gladly have filled himself with the pods that the pigs were eating; and no one gave him anything. But when he came to himself he said, 'How many of my father's hired hands have bread enough and to spare, but here I am dying of hunger! I will get up and go to my father, and I will say to him, "Father,

I have sinned against heaven and before you; I am no longer worthy to be called your son; treat me like one of your hired hands.'" (Luke 15:14–19)

RESPONSE 1

He fails. His experiment collapses. His foray into a life of lusty fullness eventually leaves him empty. He leaves the disciplines of home and family and responsibility and, like so many before him, he falls on his face. Like so many who want to stand alone, independent rocks of strength, when the hard times come, he finds no one to lean on or to cling to or to bear him up, and he ends up with swine and humiliation and the lessons of hardship that this hard world is always only too willing to teach. On his own, he gets hungry.

And then, we are told, "He came to himself," meaning he got hungry enough to swallow his pride. He decided his independence wasn't worth the price of his suffering. The emptiness in his stomach began to hurt more than the humiliation in his heart. And so he rehearses a little speech meant to touch the heart of the father he had rejected. Maybe he is sincere in his repentance, or maybe he is just desperate enough to act out some humbling little scene calculated to bring tears to the old man's eyes.

RESPONSE 2

How desperate do we have to be to turn our lives back to their source and try to go home again? How lonely do we have to get before we open ourselves to the heart of this universe and invite in the grace we are offered? How much must our spirits ache with hunger before we choose to leave this far-off country of greed and ambition and lives filled with the emptiness of all of the "stuff" we have acquired? How much stress do we have to be under before we seek the simplicity of a God who can care for even the least of us?

READER

"So he set off and went to his father. But while he was still far off, his father saw him and was filled with compassion; he ran and put his arms around him and kissed him. Then the son said to him, 'Father, I have sinned against heaven and before

*you; I am no longer worthy to be called your son.' But the
father said to his slaves, 'Quickly, bring out a robe—the best
one—and put it on him; put a ring on his finger and sandals
on his feet. And get the fatted calf and kill it, and let us eat
and celebrate; for this son of mine was dead and is alive again;
he was lost and is found!' And they began to celebrate."*

(Luke 15:20–24)

RESPONSE 1

The young man walks slowly up the road, longing but dreading to
see his father's form in the distance. He expects the anger due for
his foolishness, and the old familiar lectures and the hard words
of a tough love and especially the big "I told you so." And then he
sees him. The young man quakes inside with a mixture of fear
and shame and embarrassment and hope and even the love that
just the sight of that dear old father brings to life again. And then,
on he came. That old man running and kissing and embracing
and loving and sobbing and hugging and muttering whatever a
tidal wave of joy might bring forth from a mouth so long set in
disappointment. The son starts in, as planned, with the speech
he's been rehearsing for a week and saying under his breath all
day as he nears home, but it's no use. He can't even get out all the
words before every thought and emotion he has is swallowed by a
father's joy. He is home. And that is all that matters; all that needs
to be said; because love does the rest. This moment is not about
guilt or pride or even forgiveness or grace. It is only about joy and
a love made whole again.

RESPONSE 2

What an amazing gift is the promise of faith that Jesus gives us.
We can go home. No matter who we are; no matter what we have
done; no matter how long it has been; no matter how much guilt
there is clogging up our souls; no matter what problems we have
created; we can still turn, just turn, and we will be embraced. We
have somewhere to go when every other door is shut. We have a
love that will hold us even when there is nothing lovable about
us, even when we cannot love ourselves. God is not keeping score
or waiting for us to stumble, but loving us and loving us, right
here in the pig sty of a mess we have made in us and around us.

READER

"Now his elder son was in the field; and when he came and approached the house, he heard music and dancing. He called one of the slaves and asked what was going on. He replied, 'Your brother has come, and your father has killed the fatted calf, because he has got him back safe and sound.' Then he became angry and refused to go in."

(Luke 15:25–28a)

RESPONSE 1

And then the killjoy comes. After being hard at work, as he always is, he discovers that he has been missing the party. Of course, he has spent his life missing the party. He is angry, resentful, and full of spite toward the no-good, lazy little loser who has turned up yet again to rob him of the spotlight of a father's love that he has been striving to earn and deserve for a lifetime. He feels that this little celebration is unfair, overshadowing his own earnest, labor-intensive, dutiful relationship to his father. And, of course, he is right.

The young swineherd got his share of what he was entitled to and wasted it, as the older brother always knew he would. And now, he should get what he deserves. He walked out on his father, broke all the rules, lost all the cash, ignored every bit of teaching he ever had. It isn't fair that he should now come to reapply for his share of the love when this older and wiser son has worked his faithful fingers to the bone on the old straight and narrow. It just isn't fair. The brother may be sour and serious, but, of course, he is also right. He is always so right.

RESPONSE 2

Yes, we also know this older brother, with all of his self-righteous demands, for he too is us. Especially we who sit in our proper churches and listen patiently to didactic sermons reminding us of every ought and every should at dullingly great length. We who bear responsibilities, behave like good citizens, brush our teeth each morning, and try never to be late for work; we certainly understand this true-blue defender of the status quo. We marvel at the immoralities in the world around us, decry the loose living and the erosion of family values. We see all the signs of a society in decay in so many of our neighbors, but so much more clearly in all those who live somewhere else. We hope, deep down, that God or some other force of moral rectitude is taking note and preparing a place in whatever place those people deserve to go. From where we sit, we can see what's right and what's wrong, and most of the time, of course, we are right.

READER

"His father came out and began to plead with him. But he answered his father, 'Listen! For all these years I have been working like a slave for you, and I have never disobeyed your command; yet you have never given me even a young goat so that I might celebrate with my friends. But when this son of yours came back, who has devoured your property with prostitutes, you killed the fatted calf for him!' Then the father said to him, 'Son, you are always with me, and all that is mine is yours. But we had to celebrate and rejoice, because this brother of yours was dead and has come to life; he was lost and has been found.'"

(Luke 15:28b–32)

RESPONSE I

The angry son gets a chance to have his say. He pours out his litany of injustice, labeling his brother "this son of yours." He asserts what is his by rights because he has earned it. But what he never understands is that the love of his father was a gift. He couldn't earn it, and deserving it was never the point. There is no limit on love. There will always be enough for both sons, and for both it will always be far more than anyone could ever earn. He has spent his time designing his life to please a father who only wanted him to be himself, and would have loved him no matter who he was. Almost too late, he discovers how deep his father's love can be and that he has sacrificed so much of his life within limits that were meant to be stretched and boundaries that he never had the courage to cross.

And then Jesus brings the story to an end without providing an ending. He leaves this worried father standing there with his righteous son, both hearing the sounds of the party going on. One imagines this father turning to rejoin the celebration that he so deeply feels. And now the older brother can smell the fatted calf roasting on the fire. The dancing has already begun. The younger son's laughter can be heard echoing from the walls and rafters. And there stands this other son alone with his rage, cut off by his own correctness and well-entitled resentment. But does he go in? Does he join the love feast inside, or stalk off satisfied with his moral high ground? Does he go in to enjoy the love of his father, or sit alone outside in the cold draft that he has created?

RESPONSE 2

And so the question is also posed to us. God is caring for and loving all of those we hate or distrust; all of those that we think are wrong. Do we join the party? God is loving Muslims and Hindus, atheists and secularists, and all those that do not share our beliefs. Do we join that party? God is rejoicing over the hint of transformation in the life of a drug addict and a rapist and a murderer. Do we join the party? God wants all those peoples and races who have been put down and oppressed to be lifted up in God's special embrace, even if it is at our expense. And these parties are not for us. All this special love of God is being lavished on others, and we can hear the laughter of that punk of a little brother echoing off the walls that surround our lives. It is hard. But do we go in?

The Raising of Lazarus

READER

Now a certain man was ill, Lazarus of Bethany, the village of Mary and her sister Martha. . . . So the sisters sent a message to Jesus, "Lord, he whom you love is ill." But when Jesus heard it, he said, "This illness does not lead to death; rather it is for God's glory, so that the Child of God might be glorified through it." Accordingly, though Jesus loved Martha and her sister and Lazarus, after having heard that Lazarus was ill, he stayed two days longer in the place where he was. Then after this he said to the disciples, "Let us go to Judea again." . . . Then Jesus told

them plainly, "Lazarus is dead. For your sake I am glad I was
not there, so that you may believe. But let us go to him."

(*John 11:1, 3–7, 14–15*)

A WOMAN'S VOICE

What terrible glory of God is this?
What frightful game of cosmic manipulation leaves this man
    to die,
    just to set the stage for some holy conjuration?
How much of a price of pain does this Lazarus pay for God's
    moment of glory?
How much grief goes howling into that Bethany night?
How many tear-drenched, heart-wrenching sighs shudder
    through those sobbing sisters? The agony of death
    cannot be undone. No glory of God can undo
    these nightmare hours or compensate for the fracture of faith.
Jesus loves them? What love is this that stands by and waits
    for fear to evolve into pain and pain into anguish
    and anguish to cut into the soul—and still waits?
Save me from such love. Spare me my encounter with such God-
    awful glory.

READER

When Jesus arrived, he found that Lazarus had already been in
the tomb four days. . . . When Martha heard that Jesus was
coming, she went and met him, while Mary stayed at home.
Martha said to Jesus, "Lord, if you had been here, my brother
would not have died. But even now I know that whatever you
ask from God, God will give you."   (*John 11:17, 20–22*)

A MAN'S VOICE

Even amid the grief, Martha believes. She believes
    so much that her faith becomes a demand.
Even as she gently indicts his absence she makes the most audacious
    expectation of his presence.
She doesn't wait patiently for him to come, she goes to claim him,
    to demand the fruits and privileges of his love.
If, in Jesus, she has a direct line to God, she will use it, she
    will ask,

she will implore, she will assert her obstinate belief and
    expect Jesus
to make good on the promises of her faith.

READER
    Jesus said to her, "Your brother will rise again." Martha said to
    him, "I know that he will rise again in the resurrection on the
    last day." Jesus said to her, "I am the resurrection and the life.
    Those who believe in me, even though they die, will live, and
    everyone who lives and believes in me will never die. Do you
    believe this?" She said to him, "Yes, Lord, I believe that you are
    the Messiah, the Child of God, the one coming into the world."
                             (John 11:23–27)

THE WOMAN'S VOICE
    His words take one's breath away.
    Could it be that there is a hope beyond hope, a power
        beyond even the terror of death, a restoration that his love
        can make of what is already lost, broken and dead?
    Is there a grace in him that can take these pieces of a shattered
        heart
        and make them whole again; that can take these shadows of a
        bottomless anguish
        and turn it into new life and renewed love?
    Beyond all of the realism, the hard-headed, hard-hearted,
        practical expectations learned through decades of disappoint-
        ments, his words,
        just his words, almost make us believe in miracles again.
    His phrases of promise get to us. There is a resurrection here,
        at least,
        of that bit of dreamer and hoper and stargazer in us.
    "Though he die, yet shall he live." Do we believe this?
        No, of course not;
    Dead is dead. The moving finger writes and then moves on.
        We know
        how the world works; there's no such thing as resurrection. And
        yet . . .
    Sure, we believe, right in the sinking middle of our unbelief. Sure,
        we will hang

on to those words with every sinew of imagination we can
muster,
for there is nothing else that can wipe away the tears or lift
the deadness from our days. In our despair and pain, he speaks,
And the dry bones of faith spring up again and dance in our hearts.

READER
*When Mary came where Jesus was and saw him, she knelt at
his feet and said to him, "Lord, if you had been here, my
brother would not have died." When Jesus saw her weeping,
and the Jews who came with her also weeping, he was greatly
disturbed in spirit and deeply moved. He said, "Where have
you laid him?" They said to him, "Lord, come and see." Jesus
began to weep.* (*John 11:32–35*)

THE MAN'S VOICE
Mary comes to him and greets him with nothing but her agony.
She falls at his feet. She is beyond even the reach of his magic
words.
She too speaks of his absence, but from her it is not an
indictment, but only a cry
of pain and a glimpse into the grief of the world in its
eternal macabre
dance with mortality. And so,
He weeps.
For this and this alone he could be our savior. Because here, at
this moment,
he does not speak. He gives no sermon on faith. He tries not
one word
of comfort or empty solace. He asks nothing of her,
Not even belief. He doesn't even try to pull her to her feet.
He weeps.
He has no other answer, no other response to pure anguish.
And in that and that only we suddenly know that he understands
this human struggle with the endless loss and passing away of
everything
we love or care for; the unfathomable anguish of each love
being torn asunder, hearts aching again and again;

The thousand griefs and pains
that are present in every grief; the vast yawning of loneliness
that explodes with every new assault of death.
He understands.
He weeps.

READER

Then Jesus, again greatly disturbed, came to the tomb. It was a
cave, and a stone was lying against it. Jesus said, "Take away the
stone." Martha, the sister of the dead man, said to him, "Lord,
already there is a stench because he has been dead four days."
Jesus said to her, "Did I not tell you that if you believed, you
would see the glory of God?" So they took away the stone.

(*John 11:38–41a*)

THE WOMAN'S VOICE

The terror.
The stone is rolled away, slowly
on the very mystery of life and death. Men strain
to push it back, inch by inch,
And the gloom behind it beckons and grows.
Lazarus has been dead for four days. There are some graphic scenes
of death's grip that we do not really want to see,
or smell. Death in the nostrils will linger there
until it becomes our own. Please, do not make us come face to
face
with that specter that haunts the tomb as it haunts our lives.
Please, let us hear the words of eternal life and believe and not
believe
and wonder and speculate, but do not bring us here to the lip
of this abyss. Do not make us look into that cave or smell its ripe
message of doom. Do not make us test our little faith
against whatever is behind that stone at the boundary of our
minds.
Perhaps you should leave us, dear weeping Christ, with the grief
that we know.

Reader

*And Jesus looked upward and said, "Father, I thank you for
having heard me." . . . When he had said this, he cried with a
loud voice, "Lazarus, come out!" The dead man came out, his
hands and feet bound with strips of cloth, and his face
wrapped in a cloth.* (John 11:41b, 43–44a)

The Man's Voice

Surely a ghastly and frightening sight it was, to see this living,
   plain-daylight sort of ghost walk out of that tomb.
Did the sobbing sisters embrace him, with cries
   of joy, shouting hallelujahs and praising the power of God?
We don't know.
Maybe they just stood back, stunned, speechless, unable to feel
   anything with which to respond. Was he their returning brother,
   or some new creature forever stained with the gloom from which
      he emerged?
And what did the others think, as they stood agape and tried not
   to even move
   in the presence of a power so beyond imagining?

The Woman's Voice

Surely there were others there who had known such grief, widows
   still aching from the memories of the arms that once held them,
      mothers
   still remembering the feeling of holding the lifeless bodies of
      their precious babies.
Did they cry out at the injustice of this extremely selective miracle-
   working?
   Where is my husband, or my wife, or my child?
   Wasn't she good enough or chosen enough to demonstrate
   God's fearsome glory?
If God has the power to take away the sting of death, where was it
   when I was crying out
   in desperation and devastation? Where was it
   when I prayed and hoped and believed?
Sovereign, didn't you love me enough to respond, to weep, to save
   me and mine
   with this grave-robbing miracle of compassion?

READER

Jesus said to them, "Unbind him and let him go." (John 11:44b)

THE MAN'S VOICE

But where was he to go?
Could there be any welcome back for this battle-scarred veteran
    of combat with the grim reaper? Didn't he still stink
    of corpses and have some eternal shadow around the eyes?
Where does someone go who has seen the heart of the abyss
    or already strolled the elysian fields of eternity?
How does one pass the time of day with a neighbor after seeing
    the face
    of God or tasting the emptiness of extinction?
Who will embrace him or understand him or know anything of
    what he feels?
Will he not long for the grave again?

THE WOMAN'S VOICE

Yes, resurrection came and went, but the mystery remained. Life
    and death intermingle, and God weaves a thread through it all.
We live. We die.
We love. We sin.
We ache. We wonder.
We believe and we doubt.
God is in it all.
And all of it agonizes toward that grace beyond imagining
    where life and death are one, where understanding blurs,
    but love holds us and we fear not.

———

Holy Week
The Coming of the Sovereign (Palm Sunday)

SPEAKER I

Just a few dozen were there at the gate,
Waving branches of palm in the breeze,
Calling him king,
Laying their devotion at his feet.

It was not a real impressive crowd,
a rather motley sort of rabble;
beggars, children, peasants, fools.
So innocent, so needy, or so desperate
they probably didn't even know why they were there.
So innocent, so needy, or so desperate
they didn't need to know.

Who knows what they saw in him or what they sought?
Who knows how or where he had touched their lives?
But there were lights in their eyes,
And there was joy on their faces.
And he was certainly ruler of their hearts that day.

Laughs and cheers, cries and tears
Welled up from even the toughest old sinners at the gate,
A noise of joy and hope spilled out into the dusty road.

And they called him king.

CHORAL RESPONSE

Hosanna in the highest!
Blessed is the one who comes in the name of God.

SPEAKER 2

There were Pharisees and a few other fine folk there
watching coldly from a distance;

Frowning, staring indignantly at the absurd spectacle
    with self-righteous, superior eyes.
They muttered that he was a menace and a miscreant.

They looked good,
Those fine people standing there well dressed, well scrubbed,
    well mannered, well groomed.
They had just strolled down to the gate to catch a glimpse
    of the latest back-country holy man
    come to take the city by storm.
So smart, so secure, or so certain,
    They saw him for just what he was.
So smart, so secure, or so certain,
    They didn't really see him at all.

They were amused to hear this pathetic-looking figure being called
    a king.
They disdained the absurd spectacle and the unwashed rabble of
    a crowd.
They were indignant at the blaspheming words.

They muttered that he was a menace and a miscreant.

CHORAL RESPONSE
    Hosanna in the highest!
    Blessed is the one who comes in the name of God.

SPEAKER 1
    He must have looked a bit of a fool riding on that young donkey.
    A large man, barely able to keep his balance,
        his feet dragging in the dust of the road,
        as that little animal struggled and jostled beneath him.

    As the sun grew hotter, the sweat trickling down his neck,
        his travel-stained robe trailing in the dirt along with his dignity,
    He must have looked a foolish spectacle.

It was no triumphal procession, no grand entry,
　　but a paltry little protest march, as laden as the donkey
　　with symbolism and ironies almost no one understood.
No march of triumph it seemed, more of a sad joke.
No royal procession it appeared, more of a jester's parody.

CHORAL RESPONSE
　　Hosanna in the highest!
　　Blessed is the one who comes in the name of God.

SPEAKER 2
　　Ah, but for those with eyes to see, there was something else
　　　　about that figure bouncing on the little donkey.
　　There was something about his face.
　　It looked tired. His eyes
　　　　were almost closed, clouded with the tears
　　　　of some poignant and private grief that would never be shared.
　　It was the face of a human being
　　　　to whom everything had happened.
　　A face that had known all the longings and laments of love,
　　　　all the torments and terrors of a timeless agony.
　　All pain, all joy, all laughter, and all despair.

　　And yet, it was a face of great stillness.
　　For those with eyes to see, it was a face that was more human
　　　　than any other face, and so, not just human at all.

　　A look at that face could touch places in the heart a lifetime
　　　　untouched.
　　A look at that face could reach into souls buried
　　　　under generations of guilt.
　　For those with eyes to see,
　　A look at that face brought a lump to the throat, a question
　　　　to the head, a weakness to the knees.
　　To the lips, it brought a cry, a cry
　　　　that mixed joy and awe, fear and love, hope and longing,
　　A cry that seemed to rise that day
　　　　out of the very stones along the road.

Hosanna in the highest! Hosanna in the highest!
Blessed is the one who comes in the name of God!
Even the Sovereign of Israel, the Promised One.

Images from the Garden

✤

I

Four of them entered the garden on a quiet, warm, moonlit night. It was the kind of night in springtime when friends become lovers and lovers make promises. It was a night of shadows skipping after the moonlight among the rocks and flowers. But these four saw none of that. Their hearts and minds were filled with forebodings and fears and doubts.

After a tense and troubling meal, where Jesus had accused someone of treachery and almost labeled Peter a coward, the four of them had left the others behind to seek the serenity of this olive grove. No one seemed to know what would happen next, and Jesus seemed to grow more nervous as the night wore on. In the garden, he went off to pray by himself, telling the other three to watch. They weren't quite sure what to watch for. Neither was he.

He walked through the grove, focusing on the reassuring sound of his feet on the stone path; on the regular pace of his own breathing. "Is this really it?" he thought. "Is this where it all ends?" It was hard to accept that his life of searching and questioning, his ministry of confronting and exhorting, his faith of loving and hoping would all end with just a scattering of followers and a handful of disciples. He had hoped for so much more.

Yet end it must. He had managed to provoke the authorities beyond what they could tolerate. He knew how they would react. And that was indeed his point. He had tried to show people that love could be active, confrontive; that love could be militant without turning into hatred or violence. And now he had prepared the final lesson: that faith, lived out in love, could yield a courage that could face anything.

He knew that sooner or later some crowd of temple guards would come and take him. And then . . . he could only guess. Imprisonment? Deportation? Death? That was how those with power, secular or religious power, would always cope with a threat or a challenge. The powers that be would preserve their power. Challenges would be crushed. He had known that from the beginning. His work had always been on borrowed time. But now the rest of them would see the truth, where true faith and active love would most likely lead; to a cell, or to the end of a whip, or to a cross.

But in that moment, Jesus suddenly felt that he wasn't ready. His disciples weren't ready. There was so much they didn't seem to understand. Maybe he had challenged too soon; provoked the authorities before his real work was done. Maybe his crew of followers would not be enough, or would not be committed enough or faithful enough. Maybe he would go to his death and that would be that, and it would all have meant nothing.

He dropped to his knees in the center of the path. "My God," he said, "this isn't the time. They're not ready. I'm not ready. Let this cup pass. Not for me, but so that your will might be done." Then he rose quickly. He strode back through the garden with a purpose. He could still leave this place. There was time to hide, avoid the authorities, bide his time. He wasn't ready to risk death until he was sure that all was ready and done.

And then he came upon them asleep.

II

After waking them up by shouting his frustration with them, he headed back into the garden. When he had seen them, he realized that they would never be ready. There would never be any guarantee that they would carry on as he might wish; that anyone would. There was never going to be any guarantee that his life and death would ignite any spark or transform any person's life. Perhaps that was what faith at this moment was all about. Maybe they weren't up to the challenge that was about to be flung before them. But they were what he had and they would have to be enough. He would trust that God could make more of them than they could ever make of themselves.

When he had seen them lying there asleep, he had realized why he was hesitating, why he had almost run away. It had nothing to do with things not being ready. He was simply afraid. When he had seen them there asleep, he realized how alone he felt, and how scared.

Now as he came again to that spot in the garden where he had knelt, the fear was still very much alive in him. Maybe he couldn't do this. Maybe he just didn't want to make himself a human sacrifice. Was all of this worth his life? He didn't want to die for some faith that no one else seemed to understand, for some love that no one else seemed to want.

He dropped to the ground again, leaning his back against the stone wall. He just sat and tried to stop shaking. Maybe he didn't have the resolve. Or maybe he just didn't have the courage. He held his face in his hands and muttered almost inaudibly, "My God, why? Why do you put before me more than I can face up to? I'm afraid. I'm not the hero you wanted me to be. This will be no death with dignity, I'm too frightened. Please let this cup pass from me. There must be another way."

A cold sweat was running down his cheeks, mixing with his tears. He was ashamed of his own fears. He felt like a failure. He wished his faith yielded him more certainty or more comfort. God seemed so far away and his dread seemed so near. After a moment of silence, Jesus tried again to open his life up to God. He wanted to feel that spirit within him as he so often had. "God," he said, "let your will be done, and help me to find the strength to do it."

He rose slowly and silently and walked a little unsteadily back to his friends. Again they were asleep.

III

When he saw them asleep, he stopped a moment to look at those three faces; lined, weathered, tired, ordinary faces. He even laughed quietly at the ridiculous little scene of John's head dropping into Peter's lap, rising and falling as Peter snored. Some watchdogs! But he loved them and he was one of them. He felt he really belonged to these people around him and they belonged to him. He wanted to embrace them, laugh with them, dance with them, cry with them. Yes, maybe with that feeling inside, he could face almost anything, even death, if he knew it was for them.

But why did it have to be this way? There was so much left to do. He had so much he still wanted to say. He wanted to grab people's hearts and set them on fire. He wanted to sing with them and soak up their joy and share their pain.

And God, there were so many broken people; people who needed some kind of hope, some kind of healing, people who needed to feel forgiven and loved and cared about. Wasn't that what his life was for? At thirty-three years old he was courting death, when there were so many desperate, hurting people out there that needed what he could give. God shouldn't be about dying but about living.

He didn't shout this time. He awakened the disciples gently and quietly asked again that they watch. Then he headed back into the garden, smelling the balmy nighttime air, feeling the full-bodied life energy within him. Again he knelt down on the warm ground. He looked up at the big moon. He held his arms out wide as if to embrace the air itself. "My God," he said, "I will serve you in life, in joy, in praise. I will try to touch people with love, with care, with hope. Give me time. Give me a life to live for you. My God, if it be your will, let this cup pass from me and be the God of my life and not the call of my death."

Feeling a new hope and a new strength, Jesus went back across the garden one last time. And again, so quickly, they were asleep.

In that moment, as he looked for the last time on those dear faces, he knew that a ministry of healing, or singing, or forgiveness, or even love, was not enough. The brokenness was too deep. The fears were too strong. The evil was too entrenched. The hatreds were too pervasive. No. A little more light and love was not enough. Love must first prove that it could face that ultimate test. His connection to God's love must stand up to all the fears and the hatreds and the evils that life can offer. He must show that that love of God was deeper than anyone's deepest wounds, and that was deep indeed.

It was only then that he saw his old friend Judas coming towards him. "It is enough," he said. "The hour is at hand."

A Tenebrae Narrative (Maundy Thursday)
❧

I

The last few hours had seemed like weeks. That dimly lit upper room seemed like a distant memory. Washing the feet, sharing the bread, pouring the wine, praying alone in the garden—these were echoes from another time. Only the sight of his friend Judas coming out of the night was still vivid. He could still feel the kiss.

After that it was all a blur of grabbing, pushing, shoving, and being struck. There had been shouting, insults, threats, and then, worst of all, whispers. He could only guess at the places where they had taken him; a dark room, a damp cellar, a deserted courtyard. But the faces were vivid. In his mind he could still see the dozens of faces that had come at him out of that dark night. There were faces that had questioned and had mocked and had cursed.

He had felt the panic of being completely powerless. He felt himself yielding to that passive despair that he had so often seen on the faces of the poor and the outcast. He was hurt. He was tired. He was afraid.

Now, in that state, he would face his accusers. He stood, still flanked by the two that had dragged him there, in an opulent, well-lit room. Jesus knew it must be a private home, but the room was huge. It was certainly the most magnificent room that he had ever been allowed to enter. There were fine carpets, massive furniture, and a high-beamed ceiling.

It must have been past midnight, but there was no sign of weariness in this room. Everyone was tense, on edge. A very distinguished-looking older man entered with two younger men just behind him. They were elegantly dressed, well groomed, well spoken. Jesus realized that he would hear no anger or hatred here. He seemed to have stepped into another world, a civilized contrast to the rough street crowd that had brought him there. But he knew that somehow, these fine gentlemen and the things they stood for were the source of the hatred in the streets, even though that hatred would never touch them.

The proceedings were short. There was much talk that meant nothing. They asked Jesus questions. They seemed so reasonable and fair that he almost wanted to answer, to share his vision with them, to reach them. But he said nothing. He knew that his fate was sealed. This scene was artifice. It was a facade of justice, when the real power had already been wielded. He stood silent.

Near the end they asked him the big question: Would he claim to be the son of God? He left the words in their mouths. He would not give them an excuse to condemn him; that act must be on their heads.

When it was over, the three men, sitting solemnly behind a great table, each said the word "guilty" in turn. It slipped easily out of their mouths. Jesus could not help thinking that the word was but a ripple in their lives. They would go back to bed. He would go on to further hell.

The oldest of the three gave a small gesture. The two guards dragged him away, back into the shadows.

II

They led him along a covered walkway, past a large courtyard. Never had he felt so alone. As the cool night breeze swept past him, he shuddered, half from exhaustion and half from fear. He could only imagine what lay ahead of him.

Then, turning his eyes toward the scattered fires in the courtyard, he saw Peter. Dear, steady Peter. How he had longed to see that craggy old wonderful face. Suddenly, Peter looked up and caught sight of him. Peter's face went blank and pale. Even across the twenty or so yards, Jesus was startled at the change. Peter let out a gasp and then a low moan. His face contorted and twisted with some emotion that Jesus did not understand. Peter turned and ran. In a moment he was gone.

Jesus was stunned. What had he seen on Peter's face? He had looked at Peter with love, longing for love and support in return. But Peter was no longer with him. As Jesus had suspected it would happen, Peter had deserted him. The others had probably fled too.

Three years they had been together. All of them had vowed to follow him to the end. Once Jesus had thought he could reach and transform a whole people. Now he felt that he had failed to really touch even the Twelve. Never had he felt so alone.

III

When day broke, they took him before Pilate. Jesus knew of the vast evil and injustice that were perpetrated in this man's name. But incredibly, here, Jesus found someone who bore him no ill will. Pilate, with the empire behind him, did not feel threatened by a man he saw as merely a backwoods preacher who was said to perform miracles. In fact, Pilate had rather liked the way Jesus had managed to embarrass those pompous and troublesome priests.

Pilate had the guards seat Jesus across the table from him as he ate breakfast. At first he seemed to have very little interest in Jesus at all. He was amused by the situation. He was amused that the high and mighty priests had to go through him to have this troublemaker crucified. He laughed and muttered sarcastic comments as he ate.

After his meal, he questioned Jesus, seeming to have some interest in the miracles that he thought a holy man might produce. Again, Jesus was mostly silent.

Pilate finally took him outside to the terrace where a little crowd was gathered. Jesus scanned the crowd for some sign of a friend or a face he knew. There was no one.

Pilate offered to release him and said he would let the people decide. For a moment, some glimmer of hope arose in Jesus' mind. Could it be that after all of this, they might actually release him? Could it be that this was not his moment, that this was not his end? He looked out into the faces of the crowd. They seemed no different from the people he had been preaching to. They seemed no different from the people that had greeted him as he entered the city. In fact, Jesus became convinced that he recognized a tall, gaunt man with a scar on his face as someone that he had healed a few days earlier.

Pilate walked to the edge of the terrace. He shouted, "This man has done nothing deserving death. Shall I release him?" There was silence. Jesus looked at the gaunt, scarred man in the center of the crowd. The man looked back, along with all the others. Suddenly, from the back of the group, one man shouted out, "Crucify him!" In a moment the rest began to join in the cry, "Crucify him!" Jesus watched as the man with the scar also opened his mouth and shouted, "Crucify him!" Jesus felt a shudder of pain. Tears welled up in his eyes. Not the priests, not some malevolent Pilate, not his enemies would put him on the cross, it would be the people. It would be the people he loved, the people he had so tried to save, the people for whom he had risked his life. The people would be the ones to hang him on a cross.

Pilate offered two more times to release him. Two more times the crowd replied with one voice, "Crucify him!" Each time the words were like nails driven into Jesus' soul. Finally, Pilate threw up his hands. He turned to the soldiers and told them simply to take Jesus out with the others to be hanged that day. Pilate shrugged as they hauled Jesus away, saying, "It's not my business." Then he went in to wash his hands.

Outside, as the sun rose upon the new day, the despair in Jesus grew. He wept.

IV

It was a broken man that they led away from Pilate's chambers. Jesus had survived the beatings. He had survived the scorn of enemies and of the rich and powerful. He had even survived seeing Peter run from his sight. But now, his very own people had condemned him. Ordinary people from the streets had looked upon his face and called for his death. That had broken him. He was glad now that it would soon be over.

In that state they led him into the courtyard of Pilate's palace. All of the soldiers gathered around. They were young boys, most of them, from Italy, from Greece, from Gaul. They were far from home, surrounded by hostile foreigners who practiced a strange religion and acted superior. Like most soldiers, too young to understand why, they had been trained to make war, trained to kill. They had been trained to block out such emotions as compassion and pity almost before they had learned to feel them. And so, given the chance to vent their contempt and their anger on the foreigners who hated them, they did it to the fullest.

As a joke, they pressed a crudely fashioned circlet of thorn branches onto his head. Along with that mocking crown they hung a foolish sign around his neck and paraded him about. They spat on him. He felt the thorns pierce his skin. The blood trickled down his face. He tasted it on his parched lips. Then he felt their spit and tasted that as well.

Then, worst of all, he heard their laughter. He tried pathetically to cover his ears. They laughed louder, enjoying the spectacle of a grown man reduced to nothing.

The soldiers who were the designated executioners that day stripped him and led him away. Behind him the laughter still seemed to grow, and grow harsher.

V

He could barely walk. The soldiers laid the heavy crossbeam of the cross on his shoulders. He walked a few feet and stumbled and fell.

They laid it on him again. Again he fell. There was no strength left in him. They grabbed a man out of the crowd along the road and forced him to carry the beam and pushed Jesus into line behind him.

The hill was just outside the city. There was almost always a cross or two up there bearing a thief or a murderer or a political enemy. Even on this day Jesus would not die alone.

He looked up as he climbed the hill. Sweat mixed with the blood and spit on his face. There were two prisoners already hanging there. He saw the agony on their faces. His body was already racked with pain, but still he wondered how the nails would feel, how his flesh would rip as he hung there, how long the agony would last before he would find the relief of death.

As he reached the spot where they would hang him, looking off into the distance he saw the women. His mother was there, and Mary and Martha. They were too far away for him to see the love or pain on their faces, and he was beyond any comfort that could have been found there.

He was still gazing down the hill as they laid him down on the cross. When they struck the first nail, the shock of pain cleared his head. As the other nails found their places, he found that physical pain was almost a relief, taking his mind off the ache inside. As the warm blood ran down his hands and feet, he was amazed at how quickly he could almost feel the warmth of life draining from him.

With one heave, they hoisted the cross upright. The pulsing wave of pain, for a moment, blocked out everything. Everything went dark.

VI

He hung there. The pain was more than he could bear and yet he remained alive. The sickness he felt inside him was beyond despair, and yet he did not die.

So this is where it all ends, he thought. I preached and no one heard. I brought healing and no one cared. I loved and I ended up being hated. I tried to make a difference and nothing changed. I thought that some believed and yet here, at the end, I am alone.

In the midst of these thoughts, Jesus realized that not since those moments in the garden had he really had a moment to pray. Through this whole ordeal of horrors he had felt so alone that even God had not seemed to be with him. His whole life he had preached faith and trust in God and when it mattered most, even he had found God too far to help or to reach. Where was God now?

He had always known the risks involved in the radical message that he preached. He had always known that this sort of death was probably where his confronting and pushing the authorities would get him. But he had trusted in God that, along the way, he would have some impact. He had trusted that he was giving of his life in a way that would make a difference. He had always had faith that a life lived for God would transform other lives and change the world. Now he felt that he had been wrong. He had failed. He had changed nothing.

But Jesus felt that it was not his failure alone. If he had failed, God had failed. Why? Why did God stand back and allow such pain? Why did God remain aloof while even those who believed and loved and cared got hurt and murdered? Why did God not reach out when it was always the poorest and the weakest and the most faithful who bore the pains and the suffering. Why?

And then, for the first time since the garden, he lifted up his head, even though it was beyond his strength. He lifted up his spirit even though it was beyond despair. And he prayed. He spoke his pain to God. He spoke his indictment to God. He spoke his broken life to God.

"My God, my God, why . . . why have you forsaken me?"

The bitter, stinging words themselves seemed to give him strength. He felt now as if his very heart would break as he raised up his last effort and called out, "My God, my God, why . . . why have you forsaken me?"

His head sank down onto his chest and almost miraculously tears again fell from his long-dry eyes. Some clouds rolled across the sun, and the day grew very dark.

———

The Seven Last Words of Christ
(Good Friday)

✣

I

READER

It was nine o'clock in the morning when they crucified him.
(Mark 15:25)

Meanwhile, standing near the cross of Jesus were his mother, and
his mother's sister, Mary the wife of Clopas, and Mary Magdalene.
When Jesus saw his mother and the disciple whom he loved
standing beside her, he said to his mother, "Woman, here is your
son." Then he said to the disciple, "Here is your mother."
(John 19:25b–27a)

RESPONSE

On the scaffold of his execution, he looks on his mother's face,
    twisted in pain and fear, already set
    in the unmistakable mask of grief.
She is wailing at the unthinkable end that he invited, to her horror,
    with his own passion for confrontation.

He must have felt a poor son.
A life of traipsing after a dream of destiny and a fury of faith
    turned desperately dark.
She must have wanted a simple child of devotion; a local boy
    made good in ordinary ways;
    weekends home for dinner, wife and kids in tow.

He must have broken her heart a hundred times.
Living on the daring knife edge
    of risky ideas and dangerous enemies,
He owed allegiance only to a father in a heaven
    beyond her grasp;
And not to her, in a home empty
    of his laughter and love.

Maybe she'd been mourning him for years.
Maybe she sensed the greatness in him,
    felt the stirrings his words left in their wake,
    but in it all,
She must have known that he was not hers.

She followed in the shadows of his travels
    making do on the leavings and leftovers of his heart,
A heart offered to restless crowds instead of a family and home.
But here he was, with dying breaths,
    turning his face to her at long last
    and offering her a gift,
Surely, the dearest thing in his life.
The beloved disciple;
    bosom friend, heart of his heart,
    soul mate, fellow wanderer after dreams.
That would be his parting gift to this wailing woman
    again left painfully behind.

Everything he had failed to be as a son,
    he wished her now in his beloved friend.
And to his orphaned comrade, what more could he give
    but this lady of grace
    with years of carefully stored love
    forever unspent on a son she could caress now
    only with her bleared and swollen eyes.

Dear and brokenhearted mother, take this other son,
    for he needs the love you have so abundantly,
And he can give you the one love
    that was beyond the power of even a Christ to bestow.

II

READER
Then Jesus said, "Father, forgive them; for they do not know
what they are doing."   *(Luke 23:34)*

RESPONSE

At the end, he asks that we be forgiven.

God knows, we have much to be forgiven for;
All of the things we've said or done
    In flashes of anger
    or in moments of self-righteous judgment;
The failure of nerve
    when prejudice needed to be confronted or when cruelty
    could have been prevented;
The guilty secrets of our hearts
    of big lies and little ones,
    of betrayals and promises unkept.
God knows, we have much to be forgiven for.

In our guilty world,
    where the meek continue to be victims,
    where the children of God continue to starve and be abused,
    where the idealists are ridiculed,
    where the vulnerable are hanging on crosses of poverty;
Love is still crucified every day.

And yet, at the end,
    in his own pain, our betrayals ringing in his ears,
    his own life a casualty of our hardness of hearts,
He asks that we be forgiven.

He says we know not what we are doing.
He pleads our ignorance.
He gives us the benefit of every doubt.

Certainly, ignorance we have aplenty, as we blunder about
    in the night that comes when we close
    our eyes to the light.
But as we contemplate those
    gathered around that ancient cross, and our own lives
    as we gather around it again,
Perhaps our sinking suspicion should be
        that we know exactly what we are doing.
And we do it again and again.

Today, we need his prayer more than ever,
  and the grace of mind and spirit from which it came.
Yes, our God, forgive us.

III

READER

One of the criminals who were hanged there kept deriding him and saying, "Are you not the Messiah? Save yourself and us!" But the other rebuked him, saying, "Do you not fear God, since you are under the same sentence of condemnation? And we indeed have been condemned justly, for we are getting what we deserve for our deeds, but this man has done nothing wrong." Then he said, "Jesus, remember me when you come into your reign." He replied, "Truly I tell you, today you will be with me in Paradise." (Luke 23:39–43)

RESPONSE

There were two others on crosses that day.
Who knows what heinous crimes or petty offenses
  earned them this badge of judicial status?
But here, sharing the same pain, looking
  so imminently into the same abyss,
One uses his last gasps to taunt and torture.
Even here on this grim gallows
  in his final hour,
He finds nothing in his heart of hearts but bile
  to spill out into the dusty air.

But the other
  on his day of days,
  finds something else in the depths of his draining life.
Maybe his whole life was a horror ride of violence and mayhem.
Maybe he robbed and cheated
  and raped and burned, but here,
In this one penultimate moment, he discovers
  this odd, spontaneous
  outburst of faith.

It seems to come from nowhere.
Out of some deep
    pocket of grace beneath the guilty shadows of a life gone sour.
He follows, for once, that one basic human instinct
    to comfort a suffering fellow.
He finds a fragment
    of compassion that he probably didn't know was there
Until, staring the grim reaper in the eye, he grasps
    for some human touch beside him, and lo and behold,
    he finds his heart.

He discovers his soul. He stumbles
    upon the improbable gift of faith.
And that one moment is enough.
One grain of faith is enough.
One act
    of kindness redeems the whole sorry mess of his life.

He is a participant in a miracle that day. And the miracle
    is not on the cross beside him, it is not in the presence
    of a Savior nearby, it is the presence
Of that Savior in his own soul.
He is the miracle;
Grace for guilt, hope
    for despair, courage
    for fear, faith out of emptiness.
Condemned a lost and wasted criminal, he will die
    a surprising, unlikely saint, touched by a spirit not bound
    by any cross, transformed by a life
    beyond the reach of death.

IV

READER
    After this, when Jesus knew that all was now finished, he said
    (in order to fulfill the scripture), "I am thirsty." A jar full of
    sour wine was standing there. So they put a sponge full of the
    wine on a branch of hyssop and held it to his mouth.
                                 (John 19:28–29)

RESPONSE

Amid all the agonies of the most painful death
a ruthless empire could devise, it is thirst,
and thirst only, that moves him to words.
But perhaps, thirst was always his problem.
He went on a spiritual quest thirsting
after the knowledge of God.
He wandered in the wilderness thirsting
for a mission and a moment.
He thirsted for justice. He thirsted for love.
He had this grand, unquenchable
thirst, for a new kind of world and a new vision of faith.

And even here, even at the end, his thirst
for life, his thirst for God has not ended.

Here, as his life begins to ebb away, it is vinegar
that they push into his mouth.
His last taste is a bitter one, a taste of dregs
gone sour and rancid with his hopes.
He will take his thirst all the way to the grave.

V

READER

*From noon on, darkness came over the whole land until three
in the afternoon. And about three o'clock Jesus cried out with
a loud voice, "Eli, Eli, lema sabachthani?" that is, "My God,
my God, why have you forsaken me?"* (Matthew 27:45–46)

RESPONSE

It is a strange and eerie
cry of loneliness and despair.
Forsaken!
Is there a more desolate word?
We struggle to hear it; we struggle
to accept it.
Even he, even the one we call Christ, even he feels forsaken.

The man of God,
   this life lived every moment in God's sight, in God's favor,
How can it be that he too is forsaken?

Of course, we know such moments. When the very foundation
   of our lives crumbles, when we sit awake
   at three a.m., head in hands, heart
   racing with the unbearable tension of a hurt so deep
   it seems to be built into our bones;
When grief is so far beyond tears that we seem hardly present
   in the numbness;
When the grief is so deep, even moving
   an eyebrow seems a breakthrough; yes,
We know such moments. There are times
   when God is a distant rumor, and faith and hope are beyond
   remembering.
We know what it means to be forsaken.

But him?
The chosen one, the son of God, the Word
   of eternity; he too knows
   what it means to be forsaken?

He hangs on that cross and he
   lets out that terrifying cry, and then,
   and there, he finally reaches us.
Then and there we suddenly know him.
We can skim through the sermons, and yawn
   through the miracles, it's all just Sunday School
   up to here, but
This cry of forsaken agony we hear,
   it touches us, it echoes
   somewhere beyond our churchly intentions.

This man crying from the cross
   is no stained-glass icon, no holier-than-thou
   image of perfection, this man
   is us.

This forsaken soul is crying our pain and facing our death, and
    assaulting
the same unheeding God who leaves our prayers
cold and empty.
But this forsaken cry is also a prayer.
He lifts his head and lifts his soul and cries
    to God, even his forsaken curses.
His lowest moment is still a prayer.
Even this indictment of God's absence is shouted
    with a faith in God's presence.
A prayer, even of despair,
    is a song of hope.
A cry, even of desolation,
    is an act of faith.
In that too he reaches us, as he reaches God.

VI

READER

*Then Jesus, crying with a loud voice, said, "Father, into your
hands I commend my spirit."*   *(Luke 23:46)*

RESPONSE

The spirit of fire that drove his life of passionate longing, now
    turned to no more than smoldering embers, he surrenders
    to the one he calls Father.

Father, into your hands . . .

All those authorities, flexing their judicial muscle to take his life
    from him, all those basking in the glow of the power
    of the state, the power of life and death, all those forces
    of fear and coercion, stop here.
Their power ends at this point.
He gives the gift of his spirit to God
    just as it was given to him.

No one can take anything from him, no one
    can rob him of his dignity, no one
    can control him through fear, no one
    can wield the power of death,
Because that power is conquered in these few words.
His life was a gift, and now he gives it back.

Father, into your hands . . .

Can it be so simple?
All our strife and stress, all our competing and coveting, lie empty
    before these words.
The mystery of life is here, in giving way
    to a will beyond imagining, in allowing the power
    of life and love we call God to work
    in our will, to be our final word, and to receive from us
    this gift that is only miraculously ours to give.

Father, into your hands . . .

The meaning of our living doesn't depend
    on filling our days with busy-ness.
The dignity of our lives doesn't depend
    on anything that we do or fail to do.
The meaning and dignity come in knowing that this spirit in us
    is the gift of God.
Death cannot touch it.
Our own failures cannot diminish it.
No one can ever take it from us.

Jesus will die, but not at the hands of some executioners,
    not as punishment for some trumped-up charges,
He will die because God receives his gift.

Father, into your hands . . .

READER
When Jesus had received the wine, he said, "It is finished."
Then he bowed his head and gave up his spirit. (*John 19:30*)

RESPONSE
So it all comes to an end,
In a place called the skull,
    smelling of corpses, the wails
    of the tormented punctuated by the shrill
    cries of the carrion birds circling overhead.
A journey has reached a painful destination.
A task has come to a grim completion.

What does it mean?
Did he die here feeling the forsaken failure,
    having expected some other, more miraculous ending,
    his life simply finished and done?
Or did he close his eyes that last time
    feeling peacefully secure in a job completed,
    a task well performed and now finished?
Or perhaps the numbness of imminent death creeping
    through his limbs was just as much a wonder
    and a mystery to him as it is to us.

Maybe this finishing moment of death was a welcome relief
    and a fearsome specter,
    a triumphant sacrifice and a pitiful loss,
    a predestined fate and a terrifying surprise,
    all at the same time.
An enigma of death
    to match the unknowable mystery of his life.

Perhaps he died, as we die, with a sigh
    of fearful longing before crossing
    that sacred boundary beyond the farthest star
    of our own imaginings.

Only then could he be our Christ;
  having traveled the road of faith all the way
  to its last ambiguous turn at the horizon of life.
Only then could he be a true companion
  for our own painful journeys and trembling steps
  over inner thresholds.
He finished the task.
He completed his wondrous trek through this human
  wilderness all the way to the unknown and mystical end.
And so, wherever we venture, whatever strange path we take,
  he has been there before us, and there has found God.
Whatever pain, whatever private agony grips us,
  he has been there before us, and there has found God.
However hopeless or desperate or desolate seem our days or our
    futures,
  he has been there before us, and there has found God.

He looked death directly in the face
  and said simply,
It is finished.

Easter

The Empty Tomb

READER
*When the sabbath was over, Mary Magdalene, and Mary the
mother of James, and Salome bought spices, so that they might
go and anoint him. And very early on the first day of the week,
when the sun had risen, they went to the tomb. They had been
saying to one another, "Who will roll away the stone for us
from the entrance to the tomb?"* (Mark 16:1–3)

RESPONSE

He was dead. And it was a hard task that got them up before first
light that morning. They were looking at the dawn through eyes
still swollen and red from the day of tears just past. They had that
hollow feeling that comes with a great loss. The ache had become
a physical thing. They were just going through the motions that
morning, minds dulled beyond thought; staving off a return of
the tears, a return of the pain, by refusing to awaken the monster
of grief in their own minds.

They ate nothing. They donned the black clothing that they
expected to carry them through the rest of their days. They silently prepared the spices and the oil. And then, not daring to
even look into one another's eyes, they set off. Three women in
black, gliding ghostlike through the empty streets, making no
sound, no murmur to dispel the trance of silent mourning that
moved through the streets around them.

They were each determined not to remember yet how much
they had loved him. They were each resolute that they would not

think of how their spirits had lit up whenever he spoke. They were each sure that they could keep the image of that precious face out of their minds until they reached the tomb. That face twisted in pain, the eyes blank with despair, had already invaded their dreams. But now they watched the stones beneath their feet, they fingered the hems of their scarves, they counted the cracks in the walls to try to keep the pain in check.

The task of anointing the body loomed in their minds as a grace and a terror. They would seize the opportunity for one last act of devotion, the chance to lovingly touch him again. Even the cold flesh they would willingly caress. Yet they each trembled at the thought. Could they bear it? Could they do it? Would it be a moment of healing devotion, or would it only provoke another round of wailing and grief? These thoughts, too, they steeled themselves to resist. At least they had something to do, somewhere to go, some focus for their grief. Seeing to the practical arrangements would be their respite from the abyss of a future without him. And so they worried about who would roll back the stone. They focused their minds on this simple question. They held the aching at bay with this simple problem.

READER

When they looked up, they saw that the stone, which was very large, had already been rolled back. As they entered the tomb, they saw a young man, dressed in a white robe, sitting on the right side; and they were alarmed. But he said to them, "Do not be alarmed; you are looking for Jesus of Nazareth, who was crucified. He has been raised; he is not here. Look, there is the place they laid him. But go, tell his disciples and Peter that he is going ahead of you to Galilee; there you will see him, just as he told you."   *(Mark 16:4–7)*

RESPONSE

And they were amazed. But saying that hardly begins to express their reaction. The tomb that was sealed is open. The body of the one they love is gone. A stranger dressed in white sits there waiting for them. They are beyond amazement.

They fear that his body has been stolen. They wonder if the disciples are finally taking some action. They are angry that they have not gotten to him first. They fear this stranger sitting there in his even stranger vigil. And, yes, somewhere in the deep recesses of their minds, some irrational thought, some small tremor of hope, barely perceptible, some fleeting resurgence of their own faith is felt.

And then the mysterious white-robed stranger speaks. Who is he, this first herald of the dawn? Is this some ordinary gardener pressed into emergency service to explain the unexplainable? Or is this what an angel looks like—not memorable enough even to rate a description? They probably don't even hear him when he speaks. If this messenger travels from heaven itself to make this proclamation of a new reality, he is strangely unable to get his point across. As is so often the case, this miracle will struggle to get a hearing, will only grudgingly be believed. With minds focused on their duties toward death, these women are not prepared to hear of new life. Locked into grief, the three faithful women cannot even begin to sense the joy of this message from the tomb. This man says that Jesus goes before them, as he always did, but they hear none of it.

READER

So they went out and fled from the tomb, for terror and amazement had seized them, and they said nothing to anyone, for they were afraid. (Mark 16:8)

RESPONSE

With the reality of death crowding their thoughts, there is no room for this unwieldy miracle to intrude. Facing a stranger with a strange message, they are afraid. In the presence of this overwhelming act of God, they are afraid. And their fear closes their minds, cuts them off from this angelic visitation. Their fear defeats the life-restoring power of God in their lives. As they flee, they choose the grief and the agony they know, leaving the words of eternal life hanging in the air.

And here is where Mark's Gospel leaves us. The tomb is empty. The promise of resurrection is spoken. But our fears are still in the way. The miracle has not really touched us. The grace offered has not been received. Jesus has gone on before us, and most of us have not followed him or found the resurrection miracle because we too are afraid to believe it. We too flee in the face of what we cannot control or understand.

If there is a resurrection story to come at the end of this Gospel, Mark leaves us to write it. He leaves us to find the risen Christ and to discover the power of God's new life going on before us. He leaves us to wrestle with our fears and to choose between life and death.

———

Three Readings for Easter Sunday

❧

DEAD AS A DOORNAIL

Jesus was dead. Like Scrooge's partner Jacob Marley, he was dead as a doornail. Dead and buried. Finished, over, done with, dead.

The disciples were sure. The women were sure. The executioners were sure. They had watched him die. They had seen him carried away and laid in the grave. It was sealed. He was dead. No ifs, no ands, no buts.

That should have been the end of the story.

Certainly this little group of disciples weren't going to carry on his work. They were probably one of the most undistinguished little groups ever assembled, for any purpose, anywhere, ever.

Now with no leader, no sense of direction, no vision of what they were supposed to do next; their cause defeated, their quest ended in catastrophe, their only reason for even being together, dead—there was nothing left for them to do but break up and head home and try to remember what had drawn them together in the first place.

That should have been the end of the story.

Think of what that Saturday must have been like for them. Someone they truly loved, loved enough to drop out of their normal lives and follow him, loved enough to take risks and walk a hundred miles and invest their whole futures. Someone they truly loved was dead.

But that wasn't all. They had dared to dream with him—dreams of grandeur, dreams of power, dreams of a new kind of world. Now their dreams were dead. And they had dared to hitch their lives, totally, to a new kind of faith—a faith that crossed barriers and cared, a faith that healed and forgave and lifted up people who had never known anything but down. Now their faith was dead.

What a day of disillusionment and defeat and grief that Saturday must have been. They must have been in shock, disoriented, disheartened, well over the line called despair. It must have been a day of cold blank stares, past the point of tears. They knew that the fullness of life was now in the past and their fantastic adventure of life and spirit was over and done and dead.

That should have been the end of the story.

It should have been the end of a story that would be little noticed and never retold.

Except that somehow, it wasn't.

Somehow, it was not an end, but the very beginning of an even bigger and more amazing tale. Somehow, death was not the last word. In fact, it was nearly the first. Somehow, the story and the life and the dreams and the faith have gone on and continued to grow. Somehow, it has now become our story.

STORIES OF THE RISEN ONE

READER 1

The reports of his appearances were many. Sometimes he seemed like a spiritual presence who passed through walls or glowed with light. Sometimes he seemed very down-to-earth. The disciples could touch him and watch him eat. Sometimes he was hard to recognize until he revealed himself, but each time he was very real for those people who saw him. And he left none of their lives unchanged.

READER 2

Mary Magdalene must have seen him first. As she wept outside his tomb he approached her, and she didn't recognize him until he called her name, "Mary." So we too recognize him as he calls our names. Matthew says the other women were with Mary when they met the one who had risen. His first words to them all were "Be not afraid." So we too hear those words whenever our lives are touched by fear and we turn to him.

Reader 3

Luke tells us how two disciples were walking down a road toward the town of Emmaus. Along the road they were joined by a man they didn't recognize who interpreted the scriptures for them. That night, in the breaking of the bread, they recognized him as Jesus, and he vanished. So we too recognize him even today in the breaking of the bread.

Reader 4

John tells of that night, back in that same upper room where the disciples gathered, so fearful and worried that they bolted the doors and shuttered the windows. Suddenly he was there among them. His first words were "Peace be with you." So we too listen when we are worried and in turmoil, shut up in our own upper rooms, for that voice which brings us peace.

Reader 5

John also tells of that strange morning on the lake when Peter leapt into the water in joy at seeing him on the shore. Peter was asked, "Do you love me?" three times. And three times he was given the charge "Feed my sheep." So we too spend our lives trying to answer that question and trying to live up to that charge.

Reader 6

But our comfort comes from the very last words that Matthew wrote. The disciples were gathered on a hilltop in Galilee and above them stood Christ Jesus, the Risen One. As the Christ laid the charge upon them to go and preach and teach and begin this fellowship of believers, he ended with the words that still echo in all our hearts. "Lo," he said, "I am with you always, to the end of the age."

THE REST OF THE STORY IS OURS

Reader 1

The rest of the story, of course, is ours.

Resurrection means that the story that began
    with a life lived for others,

a passion for a God of love and justice,
and a death on a cross,
Isn't over, but lives on.

Resurrection means that the story was carried on
in lives that made sacrifices for faith,
in people who endured suffering and conflict for love,
in visionaries who sought to change the world and make
justice real.

Resurrection means that even generations of defeat haven't ended
the tale.
All the forces of greed and ambition and lust for power
haven't stopped the flow of this story of love.
It has survived even the narrowness and divisions
and incompetence of the church.
All the power and death and prejudice of this world
have never blocked its path.

And so it goes on.
Down through all the years
that resurrected Spirit of Christ comes.

And here, now, to us.

The rest of the story is ours,
it will be the story of our response, our courage, our faith,
the bearing of our crosses.
The resurrected Spirit of Christ comes, here, now, to us.

READER 2
Resurrection means that the faith that challenged the status quo
and cried out for justice,
Is not dead, but can live on in us.

It means that the love that reached out to those who were
oppressed
and excluded and downtrodden,
Is not dead, but can live and work in us.

It means that that voice that lifted up a cry for those
   whose voices had never been heard,
Is not silenced, but can cry again in us.

It means that the dream that embraced all peoples in the
      human family
   and dared to see them as one,
Is not dead, but can still grab hold of our lives and live on in us.

Resurrection means that the courage to bear crosses
   and risk even all that we have to risk,
Is not dead or defeated, but can rise again in us.

READER 3
   To say that we believe in resurrection means that
   Our Christ is not a dead and buried memory in the past,
      but a living presence that can move our lives even now.

   Our Christ is not a law set in concrete passed down to us from
      another age,
      but a living leader who is still on the cutting edge of our lives.

   Resurrection means that Christ is still showing us a path
      and calling us to follow.

   The rest of the story is being lived out in us right here and
      right now.

   Our leader is going before us,
      our Christ is still bearing a cross,
      and we are still being called.
   How do we respond?
      How do we follow?
         Is this resurrection ours as well?

   Let us be together the rest of the story.

———

He Will Swallow Up Death Forever

꙼

READER

And God will destroy on this mountain the shroud that is cast over all peoples, the sheet that is spread over all nations; God will swallow up death forever. Then God will wipe away the tears from all faces, and the disgrace of God's people God will take away from all the earth, for God has spoken.

(Isaiah 25:7–8)

RESPONSE 1

Perhaps it is the problem of death that is at the center of every religion. We come from beyond anything we know and in time we each return to the same unknowing. The very meaning of our days between that mysterious dawning of consciousness and that equally enigmatic extinguishing depends so much on how we come to see the context. Is this life just a way station in some larger process, or is this all there is, nothing moving towards nothingness once again? Are we due for some reward or punishment when this brief test is over, some cosmic reckoning; or is every day of life its own reward? So much about how we live our lives and what meaning we give to our choices depends on what we make of our own looming fate in the grave. Coming to terms with our own mortality is, perhaps, the central task of life. As Robert Louis Stevenson once wrote, "Old or young, we are all on our last cruise. And that makes all the difference."

RESPONSE 2

Death is the peculiar curse of life. Even those of us with a sure faith that something better comes after cannot completely escape anxiety over death's ever advancing grip on our lives. But our own death is not the heart of the curse. It is the painful truth that everything and everyone we treasure will someday be taken from us. Every bond of love will be broken by our death or that of a loved one. Every story will be forgotten as the tellers pass away. Every gift will eventually be taken away. Death swallows up everything. The sadness of that knowledge permeates even our joys.

Response 3

Even amid the talk of resurrection, celebration, and victory, the Easter message is thoroughly preoccupied with death. The readings on Easter Day are about tombs, graves, and shrouds. The message of the resurrection may be about the triumph of God over the grave, but it comes right at the heart of a story of painful death, grieving friends, entombment. The images that come with the Easter celebration are disturbing reminders of some of the worst moments of each of our lives and some of the worst fears in many of our futures. For those of us who have lost a loved one or flirted with the fringes of death ourselves, death is not an abstraction. It is personal, a very real presence in each of our lives. And while the Easter message is supposed to take away some of the pain or anxiety, supposed to reassure or comfort, it does not bring a loved one back. The loss is still loss. Death is still death, and seems stubbornly definitive. Jesus' resurrection is not necessarily ours.

Response 4

But perhaps, in the Easter message, there is one thing that can reach us even in our pain. God is love. Easter shows us what we already know in our hearts: that love is the most powerful force we will ever encounter. Resurrection is not some biological miracle; it is a triumph of the power of love. The love in which each of us is held is, in some mysterious way, more potent and more powerful than even the physical reality of death. We don't know what is beyond death, but we do know the power of love. We do know that love does not end with a heartbeat. We do know that love is a gift that can't be taken away from us. Death is an unfathomable mystery, but love can swallow up death forever and even wipe the tears from our faces.

Do You Love Me?
(Based on the Gospel of John)

❧

I

All of the resurrection appearances of the risen Christ are stories that provoke wonder and awe. You can sense the fear and amazement of the disciples. The words of Jesus are brief and piercingly to the point. He comes with a sense of purpose to set his followers back on their feet and back on the quest for faith. They say almost nothing, standing dumbstruck by the power of what is happening. But finally this last resurrection appearance in John's Gospel is different. It has the feeling of a quiet time reunited with friends. They talk and eat and even take a walk. Jesus here is once again approachable and imaginable, alive among them again as in the old times. Jesus is no startling or unnerving presence, but an old comrade come home again. For that reason it is the most precious story of them all. For we long for a grace of God that sometimes touches us gently and reassures us without the pyrotechnics of miraculous intervention. We long for a presence of God by our side, familiar and comfortable, miraculous only in the love that we feel.

II

The story starts with a group of men in a boat. Out most of the night fishing, they have caught nothing. They see a stranger on the beach who calls them children and tells them to drop their nets on the other side. And in the kind of miracle these fishermen could most heartily understand, their net fills with fish. Only then does one of them recognize the familiar walk and movement and voice and form of that stranger. Their master and their friend is awaiting them on the shore.

Peter cannot wait, and in his excitement decides to jump in and swim to shore. And then in a gesture so completely, endearingly revealing of Peter's spirit, he puts on his dry clothing before jumping into the water. Even in the midst of this spontaneous and awkwardly enthusiastic swim, even with the discomfort of sopping clothing, Peter will greet his master with humble decorum, fully dressed and properly respectful.

III

When they all reach the shore we can only imagine a hearty reunion and a happy greeting, because rather than offering some grand pronouncements about peace, or the Spirit, or marching orders for the future, Jesus simply asks them to bring the fish and to sit and have breakfast around the fire that he has kindled. And there they all sit. They must feel some of the old magic of those countless nights around the fire listening to the enchanted words with which Jesus had unlocked their souls. They must feel the same sureness that when he is by their side nothing can defeat them. They must feel again the thrill of a faith that can move mountains and now can conquer the grave. There they all sit, once again united as a band of spiritual musketeers ready to conquer the world.

Here, perhaps, the miracle of resurrection finally happens inside each of the disciples. Here the quiet grace of Jesus touches them again as a healing balm that puts the death of their faith to rest; that reawakens their confidence; that rekindles the fire of devotion that set them to following this man in the first place. Here, a new kind of spirit begins to grow in them that will be beyond the reach of defeat or despair. Here, as they sit quietly sharing a fish around this lakeside campfire, they feel Jesus' return not just to their world, but to their hearts.

IV

After breakfast, Jesus and Peter take a walk down the beach. To understand what passes between them, we must know that the Greek language in which the Gospel tells this story uses two different words that we translate as love. There is brotherly or sisterly love, a kind of family devotion that in Greek is "philos." But there is also the more abstract and more altruistic and selfless love that in Greek is "agape." As they walk, Jesus turns to Peter and asks, "Do you love me?" He uses the word "agape." He is asking if Peter has that kind of total self-sacrificing love for him. Peter's answer shows us a new man. He says, "Lord, you know that I love you." But the word he uses is "philos." Yes, Peter loves Jesus as a brother, as family, but here he is saying that he might not be capable of the kind of love Jesus is asking for.

Gone is the empty bravado of the Last Supper. Gone is the Peter who believed that he was the greatest and the most devoted and courageous of the disciples. In his place is a more mature and humble man. In his place is a wiser man who knows that he has feet of clay, a soul that can tremble with fear, and a heart that can easily be broken. He says, "Yes, Master, you know the kind of love I have for you, how human and fragile and limited it can be." In his mind, Peter must still hear the cock crowing as he answers.

V

Again, Jesus asks him the question, "Do you love me?" Again he uses the word "agape." Peter's response is the same. It must pain him to have Jesus press the point. It must feel as though Jesus is intentionally reminding him of his failure to remain faithful on that awful night of the arrest. Peter stands by his confession of the limited nature of his love, even though he must want to pledge his undying and total devotion once again.

Finally, Jesus asks the question a third time. But this time it is different. This time he uses the word "philos." It is an acceptance of the kind of love Peter can offer. It is forgiveness for how Peter had failed. It is a gesture of grace and gentle good feeling toward Peter that we can feel even two thousand years away. This time he asks Peter only for what Peter knows he can give, the simple, limited love of an ordinary man. But Peter is grieved. He so regrets Jesus' lowered expectations. He so feels his failure to be the lion of faith that he wanted to be. It hurts him to acknowledge once more the frustrating frailty of his faith.

VI

Each time Jesus gets his answer from Peter, he adds his request "Feed my sheep." He gives Peter the task of the shepherd, to care for those who still hold Jesus in their hearts. Maybe Peter will never manage to be the lion of faith that he once dreamed of being, but he is instead given the gentler task of tending, loving, feeding, and caring. Peter will not carry the torch of faith into battle with the powers that be, the way his master did. He will not confront and contend; he will not be the champion continuing to fight the battle for Jesus. That is a job that will find others. But Peter will be the heart and soul of the community. He will be the one who holds it together with his now humble love and devotion.

Jesus ends his talk with Peter by reminding him how frail life can become; how limited our time and our powers are. Again, Jesus is here the old friend, telling Peter with sadness how things are and will be. But with his understanding, he imparts the gentle grace that reminds us all that whatever else this resurrected Christ is about, he is about love. Whatever else this Christian movement would put at its center, Jesus put love. Whatever else our lives are called on to include, we are first and last and ultimately called to be people of love. Whatever the miracle of Easter may be, at heart, it is the triumph of love over everything.

VII

And with that, Jesus turns to Peter again and says simply, "Follow me."

Pentecost and the Season Following

A New Heart

READER
A new heart I will give you, and a new spirit I will put within you. *(Ezekiel 36:26a)*

RESPONSE
What do we know of new hearts or spirits?
We pass through our times, year after year, day after day,
With the same old problems,
The same old neurotic limitations,
    relationships scarred by old familiar insecurities,
    families plagued by well-rutted patterns learned
        from childhood traumas.
The same tired anxieties prey upon us from adolescence to old age,
    with us wherever we go, however far we run.
We wait to grow wiser as older
    but we never grow out of ourselves.
Fears felt on childhood playgrounds keep us cowering
    behind the wrinkles of middle age.
We find no escape from the companionship
    of the inner demons who dominate our days.

We try self-help books and support groups,
    hypnosis and exercise machines,
    TV preachers and transcendental gurus,
    shrinks, quacks, and snake oil.
Looking for a new me and a new you,

A new start, a new age, a new life.

But we are not new.
We are not transformed or transfigured, transmuted or transported.
We are just us.
So very much like yesterday.

READER
A new heart I will give you, and a new spirit I will put within
you. *(Ezekiel 36:26a)*

RESPONSE
Could it be possible?
Is there some power around us or within us, among us or
    between us,
      beyond the cynicism, beyond the sway of guilt and insecurity
      and fear?
Is there some power that can make something new,
      that can create something fresh out of the tired old material
      that we are?
Don't we ache to break free from the bars we have fashioned
    out of the countless mistakes of our flawed lives?
What would it mean to have a new heart for the battered, stretched,
    and toughened model
    that beats out the broken rhythm of our days?

READER
And I will remove from your body the heart of stone and give
you a heart of flesh. *(Ezekiel 36:26b)*

RESPONSE
Yes, stone it is,
And yet, would that it were only stone, cold and hard,
    without the agonies, without the continual breaking pain.
Our hearts are twisted by so many greeds and so many guilts.
Our hearts are hardened by so many assaults of cruelty and blows
    of disappointment and grief,
      hardened by the competition, the clawing for our own place in
      a land of hard hearts.

But, my God, they still get broken
and it still hurts in this heart of stone,
So many loves lost or betrayed,
So many dreams abandoned or sold out,
So many hopes crushed by the weight of the stone hearts around us.

So yes, help us to open these stone-hard hearts one more time
to a faith in newness, and fresh spirits, and a loving God.
Give us a new heart of flesh that can feel again without fear,
That can encompass the enormous loves of lifetimes,
That can know again the thrill of caring for every aching life
around us,
That can grow big enough for all the discarded idealism of youth
to be reborn,
Hearts that can embrace a faith in the triumph of love
and a God that creates a new future every day,
A future that is not like yesterday at all,
and where we are not just us, but new creatures of
grace and hope.

READER
*A new heart I will give you, and a new spirit I will put within
you; and I will remove from your body the heart of stone and
give you a heart of flesh.* (Ezekiel 36:26)

Two Readings for Pentecost

🕊

*Then afterward I will pour out my spirit on all flesh; your sons
and your daughters shall prophesy, your old men shall dream
dreams, and your young men shall see visions.* (Joel 2:28)

VISIONS

READER 1
Visions are hard to come by.

It's rare enough to see clearly what is real and concrete
  right under our noses.
I see things my way,
  you see the same things your way.
It is difficult to know sometimes if it is the same
  world we inhabit.

Seeing is not a simple thing.

READER 2

One day a bird ambles across the green spring lawn, chirping below my window, a dozen subtle grays and browns. There are eyes and movements of the head and tones to the chirping voice that seem to make the bird a real and whole personality—an "other" that I am encountering. Standing on the lawn is a beautiful and delicate creature filled with a life as unique and precious as my own. Yet, how many times, how many dozens of times, have birds walked or flown or hopped or strutted across my gaze and I never saw them. Usually I look and never see, never encounter, never know. Every day I see beaks and feathers and all those things that I call birds, but today with this little creature whole before my eyes, I wonder if I have ever really seen a bird before at all.
  Isaiah knew us. We "see and see but do not perceive."

READER 1

Yet, with all our shortcomings of sight
  it is visions we are offered and promised.
Visions of a world, not as we see it but as it is meant to be;
Visions of a humanity, not as it seems but as it could become.
Visions are what we are given.

The Spirit awakens in us visions that grow out of a long
  tradition of prophets and lovers and dreamers,
  that pull us and push us into God's future.

READER 2

Our faith is a pilgrimage of the heart;
audacious longings, burning passions,
  daring thoughts, living visions,

loving and freeing impulses overwhelming our souls
and filling our minds.

We are given visions of life and love and justice,
   of lion lying with lamb,
   of deserts springing to new life,
   of old dry bones growing new flesh,
   of prodigal failures still welcomed into loving arms,
   of enslaved peoples led to freedom in a promised land,
   of chains broken,
      and captives freed,
      and hungry people filled with good things.

READER 1
   The visions that we see with our faith,
      in the grace of the Spirit,
   Can become more real than anything we can see with our eyes.
   Like the bird on the lawn,
      visions of God are alive and whole,
      more encountered than seen.
   These visions touch us in ways
      that can ring our hearts like a bell,
   And lead us to serve in ways
      that fill our lives with the Spirit that makes us whole.

DREAMS

READER 2
   Dreams are at once magical, enticing worlds
      and fearful, mysterious threats.
   On awakening and telling another that you had a dream,
      the first question is always—
      "A good dream or a nightmare?"
   Dreams are both longed for and feared.
   They arise from places in us
      that we do not know or understand,
   They take us to worlds that are surreal mixtures
      of the familiar juxtaposed with the alien and strange.

Dreams bring us messages
　　that we can never fully comprehend or control,
　　messages that are at once from ourselves and beyond
　　ourselves.

So powerful are dreams that our deepest longings,
　　our highest ambitions, our dearest hopes,
　　　we collectively call our dreams.

READER 1
　　To have faith is to dream with God.

Living is not a private affair of the individual.
Living is what we do with God's time,
　　what we do with God's world.
The Spirit makes our dreams, likewise, not ours alone.
We are people called to dream in league with God,
　　dreams of hopeful beauty and fearful wonder.

God's dreams are of a world redeemed,
　　of the reconciliation of God and humanity,
　　of love being freely chosen over hatred,
　　of others' needs being as fully honored as one's own,
　　of peace being taken as seriously as we take our
　　　preparations for war,
　　of care being extended beyond barriers
　　　of class and nation and race.

READER 2
　　God's dream is not to be alone,
　　　to have humankind as a partner
　　　in the drama of continuous creation.

To fully live our destinies
　　as people created in the image of God,
　　God's dreams must be our dreams.

We can either live out a nightmare,
   or share a dream of hope
   with God's very Spirit dreaming, visioning,
    aching, caring, and hoping in us.

A Cloud of Witnesses

I

There is a cloud of witnesses around each of us.
As we live and act and make decisions,
   all those others move with us,
   all those whose lives have touched and influenced ours.
The more crucial our moments are
   the more those silent watchers are present.

When I stand at the edge of a choice
   where the meaning of my living hangs in the balance;
That young mother is here,
   just as she looked when I took my first step
   responding to her urging love.
That old third-grade teacher is here,
   smiling just as she did all those years ago
   when I finally understood multiplication.
That little old man is here, barely remembered;
   he once gave me a quarter for the candy machine
   when I had lost mine.
That little brown-haired girl with the beautiful eyes is here,
   looking just as she did when those eyes
   set my heart on fire for the very first time, so long ago.
The father, the coach, the friends, the ones I loved,
   the ones I feared, the faceless voices who wrote books of
   imagination that changed my life—
   many that I don't even recognize,

All those whose lives have made an investment in mine,
They too hang in the balance of my decisions.

If I become a murderer, I make a piece of them murderers.
If I throw my life away on trivial things,
    I make all of their living a little more trivial.
If I act in love or prove a champion for justice,
    their lives also grow a little in stature.

They have all invested a piece of their being in me.
I carry them with me.
They depend upon me to carry them well.

There is this cloud of witnesses around each of us,
    they are here as we worship God.

II

There is a cloud of witnesses that surrounds this whole congregation,
For we stand in a tradition for which lives have been given.
People have sometimes given everything
    to pass on what we are here to receive.

As we worship this day,
    Augustine is with us, confessing,
    and Martin Luther, and old John Calvin, looking rather harsh,
    The Puritans, the Pilgrims, the Pietists are praying with us.
They are all here as we use the gifts they have left us,
    both for good and for ill.

The black Christians whose faith in the face of slavery and racism
    taught all of us about a God of justice and hope.
The third-world Christians who listened to missionaries
    and now preach back a gospel that is richer
    than what they received.
They too are here with us.
All those who found strength in this gospel
    to carry on
    and to return love in the face of cruelty.
The martyrs,

all those who laid down their lives,
all those who quietly died rather than forsake
this truth that they share with us.
They are all here—
watching, waiting, wondering
what we will do with the gifts they've given.
They lived that we might have a chance to sit here
and hear some old, dusty words
and seek in those words a new life in the Spirit.
They invested all of their faith in us.
And so they are here as we come to worship God.

III
And sometimes the children yet to come are here too.

Perhaps they are our most profound judges.
For the love that we sow now
will blossom in their world more than in ours.
It is the justice that we achieve
that will make their world livable and free.
But the shortcuts we take today
they will pay for.
The hatreds we cover over or tolerate today
will be like a curse upon their lives.
Our racism or cynicism,
Our corruption or intolerance,
Our cowardice in the face of power
will be our legacy to them.

They too are a cloud of witnesses
awaiting our gifts,
wondering how much of ourselves we will invest in them,
Will they come into a world that will nurture and care
and allow them to grow and point them to some truth,
some meaning, or some God?
Or will they find themselves cut off,
cheated out of their opportunities by our misuse of our own?
In all of our choices,
our little and not so little decision making in life,

They are here,
    waiting, trusting, hoping.

We are making their world.
We are building their tradition, creating their history,
    investing in their lives.
By our grace and faith only
    shall they live.

They are a cloud of witnesses around us as we come to worship God.

IV

The past is past.
    It cannot change.
    It can only push us a little, and trust.

The future is not yet.
    It cannot create itself.
    It can only pull us a little, and hope.

We are now. The cloud of witnesses surrounds us,
    But this moment is ours.
    It all hinges on us.
We have lives to spend,
    gifts to give,
    choices to make,
    great fortunes of past gifts and future hopes to invest.

What will we do?
The turning point belongs to us,
    the witnesses are here and waiting.
What will we do?

———

Legacies (Memorial Day)

✦

We remember and honor all of those on whose shoulders we now stand. We live amidst a legacy from the past. There were those who gave their lives to follow a dream of freedom and dignity for all. There were those who committed everything they were to a vision of a land of justice and compassion. We must always remember that we stand where we stand not because of our own strength or courage, but because generations before us cared enough to give us this legacy of peace. We must indeed give thanks to our forebears for all of the moments of truth, the acts of courage and justice, the instincts of fairness, the gifts of self-sacrifice, and the rare moments of love.

But let us not romanticize our history or idolize our nation or deify our flag. Remember also that the past of our nation and that of our faith tradition was also one of greed, arrogance, and enslavement. If we see the past for what it was, we remember a time of building and industry that was also a time of exploitation and destruction of the environment and native peoples; we remember a time of people giving their lives in battle for the sake of freedom and patriotism that was also a time of killing, hatred, and prejudice; we remember many selfless moments of giving and wisdom, but also a history of greed, egotism, and stupidity that has left us a world scarred by generations of hatred, racism, and violence. And when we rob our past of its tragedy, we rob our future of its hope. We remember poignantly those who died in wars to keep us free, but we must also remember that many people in this world still live in bondage to the fear of war and the materiel of war that we continue to provide to the highest bidder. The lessons of our history should be cause for as much humility as pride, as much repentance as thanksgiving, as much shame as celebration.

Our legacy is one of high ideals and a very mixed record of living up to them. We cheat those ideals when we glorify our past or hide from its mistakes. Let us honor the best of our legacy by recommitting ourselves to the continuing struggle to overcome the racism that divides us, to eradicate the poverty that still enslaves, to conquer the violence that poisons our common life. Let us give some of our own precious days and efforts to try to end the injustice and inequality that continue to stain and twist our national soul. At this moment, we are building the legacy that we will pass along to generations to come. Will it be a legacy that will inspire them to stand over our graves with proud thanksgiving, or will we leave behind intractable problems and canyons of misunderstanding between peoples? Can we move this national odyssey closer to the ideals we cherish? That would be the only fitting memorial to those who deserve it most.

The Pentecost Season
Words of Eternal Life
(*John 6:60, 67–69*)

✢

READER
When many of his disciples heard it, they said, "This teaching is difficult; who can accept it?" . . . Because of this many of his disciples turned back and no longer went about with him.

(*John 6:60, 66*)

RESPONSE
And so he scared off many of his followers.
All those who were drawn to his glitzy miracles, like teenagers to
    a rock star,
All those looking for a fashionable holy man with a New Age
    attitude,
All those shopping for revolutionary religious rhetoric or
    nationalistic zeal,
All of those who only skimmed the surface
    of this bottomless gift
      just backed away, or stalked off, or pretended they were never
        with him at all.

And he was left almost alone.

It must have been a painful moment,
　a soul-searching moment of doubt.
So many had seemed open to his words,
primed and ready for his revolution of the heart.
　They loved his confrontations with the experts and the authorities.
　They marveled at the healings and the other signs and wonders.
　They hung on the words of his stories and his barbed one-liners.

But then he went too far.
He tried to reach down into them and throw open the doors
　of their souls.
He tried to tear down the walls of tradition-bound religion and
　hit them
　in the heart, with the direct and overpowering shock of God's love.
He was doing heart transplants, he wanted to make them new
　people on the inside.

But he went too far,
　and their arrogant ignorance went too deep.
They closed their ears when his call got too wild and scary.
They locked their lives in fear, preferring their parochial prisons.

They left him just as we do today
When we opt for preachers with easy words and pious
　pronouncements.
We too leave him when we grab for the safety
　that the self-satisfied and the self-righteous offer us,
When we prefer those who manipulate our fears or buy our hopes
　cheap.

We crowd into our stiff and stifling churches, and if, beyond belief,
　his words happen to seep through our pious posturing
　or come to life shockingly amid our blasphemies of boredom,
We too back away or stalk off, convinced that things just went too far.
We desert him daily, whenever his impossible message does not suit
　our needs
　or his startling call conform to our fashions of faith.
It must still be a painful moment, over and over again.

READER

So Jesus asked the twelve, "Do you also wish to go away?"
Simon Peter answered him, "Lord, to whom can we go? You
have the words of eternal life. We have come to believe and
know that you are the Holy One of God."   (*John 6:67–69*)

RESPONSE

But he is not alone.
He sees the remnant dozen, frozen in place, not comprehending
    much,
    but standing fast, holding on, and keeping the faith.

But Jesus' own doubts, his hurt, his loneliness and frustration
    speak in his plaintive question: "Do you also wish to go away?"

Peter's response is a caress.

For these few it is different.
They have seen some glow of light in Jesus the others have not
    seen.
They have heard a ring of grace in his words the others have not
    heard.

What extraordinary thing can there possibly be about a person
    that moves grown, sane men to call him Christ?
Is it a weird light in his eye,
    a strange catch in his voice,
    an odd lightness in his walk?
To look at another human being and say Savior,
    to confront another living, breathing person and say Christ;
This is an amazing catapult of faith,
    an unbelievable leap of faith.
And yet, Peter says it is not faith or belief at all.

He says they know.

They stay with Jesus because in them there is this ineffable
    certainty that everyone else has missed.
That certainty is the mysterious transformation of their own souls.

They call him Savior because they have been saved by him,
   from fear and despair,
   from the endless round of empty days.
They call him the Holy One because they have found God in him,
   unmistakably gripping their lives.
They have felt the touch of God in his touch.
They have tasted eternity every day in his presence.
They don't have to believe, they don't even need faith,
   because they know,
   because it has happened to them.
Once they were lost and now they are found.
Once they were blind and now they see.
Once they had that deadness within them,
   but then he spoke the words of eternal life,
   and that eternal life happened to their hearts, then and there.

And so it can happen, even to us, even here, even now.

———

Creative Creation

READER
*In the beginning when God created the heavens and the earth,
the earth was a formless void and darkness covered the face of
the deep, while a wind from God swept over the face of the
waters.* (Genesis 1:1–2)

RESPONSE
   In the heart of that primordial abyss,
      God's Spirit moves.
   Over the face of those empty waters,
      God's Spirit moves.
   Through the shadows and the chaos
      of our own primordial times,
      God's Spirit still moves.

Through the expectant darkness in us,
   through the empty waters of our own souls,
   across the face of our own depths
      the Spirit of God moves.

That Spirit, always blowing and brooding,
   always coming, going, happening, creating.
God's Spirit is still a moving thing.

READER

Then God said, "Let there be light"; and there was light. And God saw that the light was good; and God separated the light from the darkness. God called the light Day, and the darkness Night. And there was evening and there was morning, the first day.   *(Genesis 1:3–5)*

RESPONSE

God said it and there it was.
"Let there be light" and there was light.
   Light playing across the waters
      churning with God's driving spirit.
   Colors, dancing, sparkling, shining, stunning,
      flashing, blinding light.
   And it was good.
   My God, it was good.
      Even with no eyes to see it and no sun to shine it,
   It was very good.

Maybe, good God, good enough
   for some playful cosmic smile across the face of the deep
   over the glory of it all.
But miracle of miracles,
   the night was still there too,
   one separated from the other.
      Light chasing the shadows
      and shadows chasing the light.
A playful, joyful rhythm of being
   alive before life.
And there was evening and there was morning
One holy, sacred, miraculous day.

Then God said, "Let the earth put forth vegetation: plants yielding seed, and fruit trees of every kind on earth that bear fruit with the seed in it." And it was so. . . . And God said, "Let the waters bring forth swarms of living creatures, and let birds fly above the earth across the dome of the sky." . . . And God saw that it was good. . . . And God said, "Let the earth bring forth living creatures of every kind; cattle and creeping things and wild animals of the earth of every kind." And it was so. (Genesis 1:11, 20, 21b, 24)

RESPONSE
Beyond imagining, it all came to life.
And in every miraculous moment it all comes to life again.
From slime mold to cedar trees,
From microbes to manatees,
From garden slugs to the family cat,
Life hatches and blooms, blossoms and births.
Life happens.
No cosmic reason why it should
But there it is and on and on it goes.
Creatures in their millions of kinds growing and slithering,
swimming and swarming
their way from mystery into decay.
All is change. And it never ends.

No two creatures are twins,
No two moments of life are alike,
No two places in the midst of it are the same.
It is a mind-numbing maelstrom of changing scenes and
curious creatures.
What kind of outrageous creation is this?
What kind of life-loving, belly-laughing,
mystery-midwife sort of God is revealed in all of this?

READER
Then God said, "Let us make humankind in our image, according to our likeness; and let them have dominion over the fish of the sea, and over the birds of the air, and over the cattle, and over all the wild animals of the earth, and over every creeping thing that creeps

upon the earth." So God created humankind in God's image, male and female God created them. God blessed them, and said to them, "Be fruitful and multiply, and fill the earth and subdue it."

(Genesis 1:26–28a)

RESPONSE

> And into the middle of this crazy quilt of life
> > comes one more amazing piece: us.
> The one set of creatures who have to think
> > about why they are here.
> Enough God in us
> > that we come to think that God may be in our image.
> Into this magical holy garden, we are born as comic mystics.
> > No feathers or fur,
> > No shells or claws,
> > More brains than body,
> > More heart than sense.
>
> Is this God's image,
> > The freedom, the love, the spirit, the creative passion?
> Then where did the ugliness come from,
> > The hatred, the lies, the pathetic ambitions?
> > One more unsolved puzzle we are.
> > One more mystery to live in.
>
> The one piece in all of creation
> > that can turn and love God freely;
> that can smile out an unrequired thank-you
> > just for the joy of it all.
> Also the one piece in all of creation that can turn
> > and thumb its nose,
> > and spurn the giver,
> > and destroy the whole unbelievable thing.
>
> And yet, God, nonetheless, said that it was good.

————

Jeremiah's Search

READER

*Run to and fro through the streets of Jerusalem, look around
and take note! Search its squares and see if you can find one
person who acts justly, and seeks truth—so that I may pardon
Jerusalem.*   (*Jeremiah 5:1*)

RESPONSE

Just one would be enough;
    no multitudes of saints are required;
    no sea of saviors;
    no roll call of the righteous;
    no tumult of truth tellers.

Just one was needed.
Just one tired worker
    hanging on to hope by the fingernails.
Just one passionate dreamer
    who hadn't drifted into indifference.
Just one witness to the hard truths
    who hadn't bought some piece of the big lie.

Jeremiah only needed one, and he came up empty.

He found self-righteous religion, empty with pious words and
    easy charity.
He found wealthy mouthpieces for the twisted status quo.
He found a silent majority ugly with anger.
He found many who had tried and gotten tired and given up.
Jeremiah only needed one, and he came up empty.

Now the search must go on in each one of us.

Can we find in ourselves a surging passion for justice
    that just won't let go?

Can we find a piece of hope
  so deep in the heart of us
  it forces us to believe that God can recreate
  a city of fairness and love?
Can we find, this day, a thread of faith left in us
    that is stronger than the violence and poverty of our cities;
    that is more powerful than the anesthetizing exclusivity of
      our suburbs;
A thread of faith that is deeper than racism;
  broader than greed;
  more important even than life itself?

Just that one bit of faith and hope and passion might be enough
    to save us.

When we gather for worship,
  we gather to continue Jeremiah's search
  in our own hearts and souls.
We come together, looking, listening, searching, yearning.

———

Doing Justice and Loving Kindness
(Based on Micah 6)

❧

READER
  God has showed you, O mortal, what is good; and what does
  the Sovereign require of you but to do justice, and to love
  kindness, and to walk humbly with your God?   (Micah 6:8)

I

Do justice, says Micah.
Just like a prophet, it's a tall order he gives us.

But what is justice?
Maybe it is something we feel and sense more easily than we define.

When opportunity is given to some and denied to others
    for reasons that are cruel or arbitrary,
We feel a stirring inside us.
When someone who has much takes even more
    while some are left without,
We feel that something in us is offended.
When someone weak or helpless is used or abused
    by those with power or authority,
We feel a rage grow in the pit of our stomachs.

It's an old feeling that has always been with us.
As we watched schoolyard bullies pick on the weakest,
As we watched one child punished for what another one did,
Something in us always wanted to cry out,
"It's not right! It's not just!"

And all these years of seeing a world of bullies and injustice,
    and living with it and bearing it and being part of it,
All of the years have never totally taken that cry away.
It may be dulled and lulled
    and rationalized and anesthetized,
But it is still there,
    the rage, the cry, the stirring,
    these gifts of God are still there.

But Micah doesn't say, feel justice,
    or think about justice, or cry about justice,
    he says, Do justice.

When that stirring is in us, we are called to act on it.
When that cry is in our hearts
    we are called to let it move our lives
When that rage is in our stomachs
    we are called to let it rule our choices.

There are sides to take.
There are stands to make.

There are wrongs that can't be righted without us.
There is a God who can't be embodied
   unless we stand where justice stands.

Justice is something to do.

II

Love kindness, says Micah.
For here, doing kindness is not enough.

Nice gestures, kind actions, generous moments,
   gifts of time and thoughtfulness—
These are not enough.
Our love must go with them.

Kindness can be patronizing,
   giving can be superior,
   generosity can be manipulating,
   gestures can be empty.
They come to life only when they are linked with love;
When they grow out of our deepest selves,
   our highest commitments,
   our most sacred values.

When we give our money, our effort, our goods,
   our best wishes, even our prayers,
   for others,
It is not enough,
Unless a piece of ourselves goes too.
A part of our longing, and caring, and loving must bring our gifts to life.
Our kindness must come from our center;
   our faith, our hopes, ourselves.

III

Walk humbly with God, says Micah.
Yes, whatever else it is, life is a walking business.
Nothing stays still or stays the same,
   there is nowhere to stop for long.

Life is a journey
  and our own legs, our own fortitude,
  our own energy, our own courage,
  are the things we will need to get us along the road.

We have somewhere to go.
Wherever we are right now,
It is not where we are meant to be.
We have traveling to do.

Let our faith not be a house on a solid foundation,
  but a tent we can carry with us,
  that can move and change and help us along the road.
Let our loves not be for "things" that are attached and tied down
  but only for others that can come along
  and join us on the road for a while.
Let our cares not be to hang on to what is
  or to long for what was,
  but to move along, always reaching for what might be.

We have traveling to do,
  but don't look to hop on to something for the ride,
  for then the road will only be something on the far side of a window
  and the journey won't have been yours.
And don't run—
  you'll miss so much along the way.

And remember that you never have to walk alone.
You have a companion.
You can walk with God.

But walking with God may be humbling.
For it means that when the road forks,
  you may have to go the way God goes
  rather than some other way you might like.
It means you might have to adjust to God's pace
  rather than set your own.
You might have to hurry to keep up, sometimes,
  or slow down and meet some adventures along the way.

It means walking toward a destination that you might not have chosen.

But it also means that you'll never need a road map,
    and there will be some wonderful surprises along the way,
And you'll never walk alone.

We have some traveling to do.

IV

Listen, for the words are from a prophet of God:

"Do justice, love kindness, and walk humbly with your God."

———

And I Opened My Eyes
(Based on the story of Bartimaeus, Mark 10:46–52)

❧

I used to dream of colors.
    Reds and greens would swirl in my head.
    I would see trees in my mind on fire
        with colors that had no business being there,
        vivid sky-blue leaves against a backdrop of red bark.
Knowing I would never see the external world again,
    My mind created its own internal way of imagining texture and color
        and shape.
The blindness that changed so many outward parts of my life
    transformed too the life of my imagination.
On hearing a new voice, I would give it a face of fancy
    and imagine wild grins and fierce grimaces.
    But mostly my world was a place of beauty.
    If I wanted, all streets were clean,
        all faces were perfect, all clothing was regal,
        and even I took on a princely bearing.

The realities of sight were my own to create, and create I did.

I don't know what possessed me to cry out that day at the city gate.
Certainly, my poverty was miserable enough to cry for mercy.
    Clearly, any change or any gift would be an improvement in my lot.
But for so long I was content to be just one more beggar
    in a long line of beggars.
What I wanted was clear, enough money to help me to squeak by in life.
My needs were modest, my desires dulled by years on the street.
    But that day, something was different.
When Jesus walked through the gate, something new emerged in me.
Suddenly I couldn't hold back the tears,
        and the ache, and the cries of all the years.
    I shouted and yelled and howled and no one could shut me up.
When they brought me to him, I felt completely the fool.
This time I imagined him there seven feet tall,
    dressed in robes that glowed in the sun
    with a face like a spring morning.
And there was I, dirty and insignificant, looking the idiot.

But at first, I thought it was a strange question that he asked.
    "What do you want me to do for you?"
What do you think I want you to do for me?
    I want colors and faces and light that turns the air to gold.
    I want to know what my foot is about to hit.
    I want to find the worm in the fruit before it goes into my mouth.
    I want to see again.
"What do you want me to do for you?"

And yet, no one had ever asked it before.
    Hundreds had gone by and dropped a few pennies in the cup.
    Dozens had tossed me the leftovers of their meals.
    A few had given me their old clothes.
But no one had ever asked me before what I wanted.

I don't know what I expected, but I wasn't really surprised
    when suddenly my eyes were open and the world was there.
He didn't even pause,
    he said a few words about my faith that I didn't really understand.

He walked on.
I stammered something about thank you,
    at least I hope I did,
      but I couldn't think about my mouth just then, or faith or
      anything else.
My life was suddenly in my eyes.
He seemed to understand.
    I only really saw him from the back by the time I adjusted to what
    was there.
I think he was kind of short and his cloak was dirty.
He didn't look all that much better than I did.

The first few moments were wild.
The world exploded in my face.
The light was more varied and the textures so much more subtle
    and nothing like it had been in my mind.
The view from the gate where I'd been sitting for so many years
    was a whole new world at which I had never guessed.
For a while I just ran from place to place
        looking, staring,
        gazing, peering,
        gaping, leering.
I looked in every way one could look.

But after a while, I finally began to see.
After the newness began to pass, I saw the suffering.
I saw that the world was much dirtier and the life around me
    much uglier than I could ever have imagined.
I could see the hunger and the poverty.
I could see the longing in those eyes that hadn't yet yielded to despair.
I could see those who seemed hopeless,
    and for a few of those around me,
      there was far more pain in their eyes
      than had ever been spoken in their voices.
In my mind, everyone seemed so much alike in so many ways.
When I could see, I was suddenly struck that some of us sat in the dirt,
    while others were carried where they wanted to go.
    riding on fine carpets and dressed like temples.

I saw injustice.

I suppose I should have remembered how it all looked,
    how the grand palaces towered over the crooked hovels,
    how the grand people lifted their noses in the air and looked away
        when they passed the likes of me.

How the soldiers bowed to those important people
    while they kicked my friends,
How the despair looked in people's eyes like a shade drawn over
        the soul.
But I hadn't remembered,
    And perhaps I had never really seen it before,
        but seeing again now it hit me like a wave.
    In my mind, the world had been so alive.
Now that I could see, death was all around
    and there would be times when all I could do was
        close my eyes again.

In the midst of the shout of beauty,
    the colors and the textures and the bouncing of light,
People had littered the world with such moments of ugliness and pain.

Yes, sometimes, I just closed my eyes again.

A Reading and Covenant for Love and Justice

🕊

READER 1
    I can't help but notice every day,
    I live in a land where the rich indulge
        and celebrate the glory of the American dream,
    While the poor smolder, or keep trying,
        or turn away, or still somehow manage to hope.
    The well-heeled talk of tax incentives and a growth economy,
        property values and competition,
    and this is what prosperity means.

On the other side of town, the other side of life,
the talk is food stamps and how to get by
and where to go to get off the street.
Mostly there's not much talk at all.

The differences tear at the pit of my stomach.
No matter how it's dulled and lulled
and rationalized and anesthetized—
I've got a rage, and a cry, and a deep-down hurting,
knowing that this is wrong.

But it's all too big,
and I'm too small
and the cry's not heard
and I don't know what to do.

ALL

We have a covenant with God, to live and breathe the Word of Justice; to work, to try, to cry out, and to believe the promise. The poor shall be lifted up. The oppressed shall go free. The hungry shall be filled. And God's will shall be done. We have a covenant with God.

READER 2

I live a daily routine.
I do a job and make a living,
I try to be good at what I do, move up, be a success.
The money's good, but never quite enough.
Sometimes it's a grind, a boring, dull routine.
Sometimes it's a panic, a rushing, busy, demanding pace.

I wonder at times where I am.
There's the family at home that never gets enough of my time.
There's the job that always wants more and never really leaves my
mind.
There's the church and all that good work and those big issues
that I
wish I had the energy to think about.

There are all those old private dreams and longings, the
    hundred things
I've always wanted to do that won't get done.
And where in it am I?

I make a hundred little compromises every day.
    compromises of time, of values,
    of family, of dreams, and even of soul.
I fear commitments that might fragment my life even more,
    yet I long for convictions that seem to have gotten lost
    somewhere in this routine.

I haven't sold out, I've just gotten all split up,
    and I'm tired to the bone.

ALL
    We have a Word that brings us to life and makes us whole. We are
    ministers of that Word. The touch of God upon us flings open our
    hearts and rings our souls like bells. The presence of God within
    us sets our spirits on fire and throws off our shrouds of death. We
    have a Word that brings us to life and makes us whole.

READER 3
    I know that I have public responsibilities.
    I read the papers. I keep informed. I vote.
        Every once in a while I do even more.
    I care about a better world,
        but in me there is this creeping despair over our public life.

    It is a time of the politics of pandering,
        a time of distortions and lies,
        the selling of public fantasies like laundry soap,
        and the waving of enough flags to blow the truth away.
    Our government is awash in money and media and mediocrity.
        Leadership is in the hands of poll takers.
        Ideals are put on and taken off like cheap shoes.
    And nobody out there seems to care.

Most of us are busy taking care of number one.
Most of the churches spend their time wondering
  how to fill the pews and the collection plates.
The politicians smile and tell us we are the greatest
  people in the world and the last, best hope.

How can I swim against this tide?
How can I make it different?
How can I beat back this pall of despair that anything will ever
  be different?

ALL

We have a call to proclaim the gospel; to speak the truth to power; to hear and give voice to creation's cry for justice and peace; to teach and preach and witness and tell the stories of a God that liberates and loves, challenges and accepts, reconciles and makes new. We trust that the living Word is in us. We have a call to proclaim the gospel.

READER 4

I am not a courageous person.
I have my share of fears and insecurities.
I also have my share of defenses and needs for independence.

I want to reach out to others,
  be vulnerable, be open,
  be part of the community of faith.
But I have to admit that deep down, I'm afraid of all of you.
If I allow myself to really care, I give you power,
  the power to crucify me with one cruel look or word or act.
I envy you,
  for somehow I feel that your aloneness
  is not as terrifying as mine.
I don't trust you,
  as I cannot believe that you are as broken
  and vulnerable as I am.
There is an abyss between us that is so hard to bridge.

When people are really different from me,
   whether in race or class or language or culture,
   my fears grow even worse.
I can never know how much we share,
I simply tremble before the mystery of someone
   whose experience is strange.
   Or whose world leaves me feeling outside looking in.
It is safer, easier, to go it alone, sufficient to myself.

And so, often, I don't speak out,
   or take the risks of faith,
   or live the gospel of love,
   or try enough to understand those who are different.

No, I am not a courageous person.
Yet, in it all, I ache to embrace a friend.
I long to give and receive the gifts of love.

ALL
   We have a faith that leads us beyond ourselves. We believe in a
   power of God that can overcome our fear and break down barriers and bridge the abyss. We seek the face of God in the faces of
   our sisters and brothers. We hear the voice of God in human
   laughter and human cries. We are not alone, but together on a
   pilgrimage with God before us and in us and with us. We have a
   faith that leads us beyond ourselves.

READER 5
   It seems sometimes that the whole world is at war.
   Here, there, wherever—
      the killing, the maiming, the dying, the hating,
      goes on and goes on.

   Those that aren't killing are preparing to kill.
      We are in a permanent state of mobilizing for war.
      The bangs get bigger.
      The technology of killing gets more expensive
         and more efficient.
   And anyone with any sense is scared to death.

We all wonder aloud these days,
What end will we have?
Will it be mushroom clouds, or poisoned air,
　　or a greenhouse climate or an ocean of garbage
　　or just the overflowing power of hatred and fear?

The scenarios are grim.

Must it be like this?
Must it be like this?

ALL

We have a hope that fills our future. We are called to dream in league with God. To dream of a world redeemed, of love freely chosen over hatred, of peace taken more seriously than preparation for war, of care extending beyond the barriers of nation, class, and race. We have a vision of all of humankind as partners in the drama of God's continuous creation. We have a hope that fills our future. Praise be to God.

Scripture Index